KILNAHUE CHUR(

CW01521193

A SURVEY OF THE ICONOGR.. .. .

GERRY MULLINS

GOREY CHURCHYARD HERITAGE GROUP

First published in 2011 by
Gorey Churchyard Heritage Group
Ramsfort Park, Gorey, Co. Wexford.

ISBN: 978-0-9568641-0-9

   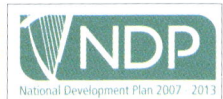

Project survey by: Michael Considine (Chairman)
                    Matt Duggan (Secretary)
                    John Nangle (Treasurer)
                    Chris Power
                    Angela Whitmore
                    Gerry Mullins (Archaeological Consultant)

Cover and dedication page photographs by Christy Farrell
Information co-ordinators Matt Duggan and John Nangle
Design and layout Gerry Mullins
Printed by Gorey Print

This publication was funded by Wexford Local Development

This book is dedicated to the Irish headstone cutters
of the 18th and 19th centuries

Welcome to Kilnahue

Contents

Page Number

Acknowledgements   vii
Introduction   viii
Location Map   xv
Site Plan   xvi

Headstone Number

1	Darcy 1767 and 1847	1
2	Rough Stone, initials MD.	2
3	Hobbs 1946	3
4	Hobbs and Kavanagh 1873, 1901 and 1913	4
5	Hobbs 1878, 1879, 1914, 1921 and 1936	5
6	Illegible Memorial	6
7	Hobbs 1818 and 1841	7
8	Webb 1868 and 1894	8
9	Brazil 1886, 1888 and 1914	9
10	Darcy 1820 and 1828	10
11	Bolger 1780	11
12	Nolan and Byrne 1847, 1852, 1865, 1868 and 1873	12
13	Keoghoe 1774	13
14	Kvghoe 1772, 1773	14
15	Cauanach (no date)	15
16	Bready 1761	16
17	Boulger and Cullen 1770, 1847 and 1855	17
18	Fitzsimons and Fitzgerald 1845 and 1888	18
19	Rough Stone, no inscription	19
20	Byrne 1890 and 1892	20
21	Byrne 1879, 1886, 1892 and 1898	21
22	Mordin 1763 and 1766	22
23	Fragmented Memorial, no name or date	23
24	Murphy 1784	24
25	R.I.P., no inscription	25
26	Murphy 1786	26
27	Murphy 1792	27
28	Toole 1770	28
29	Cullin and Daneley 1814 and 1815	29
30	Mooran 1789 and 1804	30
31	Sheridan and Byrne 1862, 1866, 1873 and 1902	31
32	Byrne 1906, 1914 and 1919	32
33	Kinceley 1779	33
34	Bulger and Dunn 1794	34
35	Dunn 1768, 1789, 1798 and 1807	35
36	Tighe 1810 and 1826	36
37	Redmond 1791 and 1834	37
38	Kinslough 1791	38
39	Connor 1769	39
40	Uninscribed Iron Memorial	40

41	Heydon 1716 and 1742	41
42	Redmond 1764	42
43	Sinnott and Davis 1818 and 1843	43
44	Byrne 1814	44
45	Keating and Kavanagh 1807 and 1808	45
46	Darcy and Flusk 1827, 1829 and 1850	46
47	Darcey 1809	47
48	Laughlin 1757 and 1788	48
49	Illegible Memorial	49
50	Aylward 1782	50
51	Doyle 1821	51
52	Kenna 1897, 1898 and 1903	52
53	Fitzsimons 1869 and 1880	53
54	Toole 1816	54
55	Rocetor 1778	55
56	Cullon and Cullin 1796	56
57	McDaniel 1795 and 1797	57
58	Dooley and Fitzgarield 1798 and 1801	58
59	O'Neill 1799	59
60	Doyle 1766	60
61	Conor 1745	61
62	Kereuan 1765	62
63	Kelley 1727, 1745 and 1762	63
64	Woodbyrne 1792	64
65	Illegible Memorial	65
66	Byrne 1773	66
67	Byrne 1744	67
68	Uninscribed Memorial	68
69	Wadic 1757	69
70	No Name or Date	70
71	Effigy of Angel, no inscription	71
72	Stanton 1773 and 1778	72
73	Murphy 1807 and 1804	73
74	Brislawn 1778	74
75	Brishlane 1766	75
76	Masterson 1727	76
77	Masterson 1738	77
78	Fragmented Memorial, no name or date	78
79	Cullen 1810, 1839 and 1840	79
80	Wadic 1743, 1757, 1767 and 1780	80
81	Uninscribed Memorial	81
82	Bolger and Kavanah 1804, 1806, 1817 and 1819	82
83	Bolger and Dempsey 1801 and 1828	83
84	Bulger 1794	84
85	MB Memorial	85
86	Breen 1787	86
87	Breen 1799	87
88	Kain 1778, 1810 and 1830	88
89	Nouland and Crean 1799, 1804 and 1816	89
90	Uninscribed Memorial	90

91	Toole and Corrigan 1776 and 1794	91
92	Uninscribed Rough Stone	92
93	Uninscribed Iron Memorial	93
94	Murphy 1894, 1898 and 1933	94
95	Hanlon 1816	95
96	Kerin 1752	96
97	Nicholoson 1844, 1845, 1868, 1877 and 1882	97
98	Cain 1772	98
99	Uninscribed Rough Stone	99
100	Byrne 1775, 1791 and 1797	100
101	Finnell / Fennell 1789 and 1797	101
102	Sinnott 1780	102
103	Dorcy 1742 and 1759	103
104	Breen 1840, 18??, and 1856	104
105	Higgins 1801	105
106	Nolen 1828	106
107	Uninscribed Rough Stone	107
108	Kinsley 1807	108
109	Kinsela 1787	109
110	Stanton 1811	110
111	Uninscribed Iron Memorial	111
112	Illegible Memorial	112
113	Byrne 1741 and 1757	113
114	Byrn 1769	114
115	Connor 1821 and 1831	115
116	Travers 1871 and 1888	116
117	Byrne and Mulligan 1812, 1832 and 1867	117
118	Kavanagh, no date	118
119	Donohoe 1880 and 1883	119
120	Travers 1866, 1880 and 1882	120
121	Connor and Redmond 1864, 1870, 1881, 1891 and 1903	121
122	Connor and Roche 1809	122
123	Richmond 1787	123
124	Woodroofe 1900	124
125	Doyle 1851, 1876 and 1887	125
126	Fallen headstone, no visible inscription	126
	Glossary of Decorative Motifs	127
	List of Placenames inscribed on Kilnahue Memorials	130
	Charts	132

Acknowledgements

First and foremost I wish to thank Fintan Kemple, Director of the Gorey Community School Adult Night Classes. His decision to promote the Churchyard Heritage course was pivotal in bringing about the formation of the group resulting in this publication.

Thanks are due to the staff of Wexford County Council for the upkeep of the churchyard. Their efforts made the task of surveying so much easier.

I would like to acknowledge Christy Farrell for providing the cover and dedication page photographs.

I wish to thank Leonie Meehan for surveying and drawing the site plan and location map.

A thank you is also due to Clare Mullins of Byrne Mullins Archaeological Consultancy for proof reading and commenting on the final draft.

It was John Nangle's idea that we should survey Kilnahue, I thank him for leading us to such an interesting churchyard.

Finally, the Gorey Churchyard Heritage Group wishes to convey its appreciation to all those who showed interest in the progress of the survey and for the help offered by Joe Millar. We thank the Doyle and Howard families for their hospitality during the course of the work and finish by acknowledging all those who worked in the churchyard before us, notably Kathleen Greene of the Explore Group and Brian J. Cantwell.

Introduction

In late 2009 I approached Fintan Kemple, Director of Adult Education at the Gorey Community School, to see if there was any interest in running a heritage course of some kind. To the best of my knowledge a similar course had not previously been available in Gorey. Fintan agreed to advertise Churchyard Heritage and wait to see what kind of a response it got. Churchyards command a wide area of study, allowing diversion into many aspects of our past. The subject therefore seemed a good option and hopefully would attract those with a general archaeological interest. As stated by John Talbot White in Francesca Greenoak's book[1], *God's Acre*:

> *'The churchyard is the centre of communal worship and celebration, the site of the most important occasions of life, baptism, marriage and burial '*

The uptake for the course was reasonably successful and it attracted a small group: Angela, Chris, John, Matty and Michael. Although everybody attending had their own particular areas of interest, ranging from general archaeology through local history to genealogy, we managed to form a congenial group. The production of this publication is the culmination of our work.

There are distinct fields of study associated with an ancient churchyard, one being the shape of the site. Many are circular, sub-circular or oval, as is Kilnahue, suggesting that they originated as Early Medieval Ecclesiastic foundations. Comparable sites are reasonably common throughout Ireland, and are celebrated for their wide variety of archaeological monuments. The most admired of these are undoubtedly the world famous sites at Glendalough and Clonmacnoise. Vast numbers of people visit these sites every year contributing to both the local and national economy. But most sites are more humble, including Kilnahue. The foundation outline of the old church is still obvious in the burial ground at Kilnahue, set in a central location. There is also a possible granite Bullaun stone on the site (Photograph 1) Traditionally the depressions in these stones are said to result from long hours of kneeling at prayer by a local saint. Water collecting in the depressions was believed to produce various cures. The Kilnahue example is said to cure warts (personal comments to Matty Duggan and John Nangle by the

Photograph 1: Possible Bullaun Stone at Kilnahue

---

[1] Greenoak, Francesca. 1985. *God's Acre*. Orbis Publishing Ltd, London.

neighbouring Doyle and Howard families). But of course it is far more likely that Bullaun stones originated as water fonts or cross sockets.

Most ancient churchyards continued to serve as burial grounds long after the church structure ceased to function. Unlike many other archaeological monuments that became obsolete in time, burials have provided a continuity of purpose to the churchyard that otherwise might have been lost. Such continued burial has allowed the archaeologist to add a further dimension to his / her previous concentration on prehistoric and medieval funerary cultures. The headstone, which was introduced into Ireland from England during the latter half of the 17th century[2], has often become the focus of this attention.

Genealogical studies possibly represent the current most popular interest associated with the headstone. Due to a history of mass emigration Irish genealogy is currently being studied world wide. Among the Irish diaspora are about forty million North Americans claiming Irish descent. Genealogical or headstone studies and the recording of memorials can only be beneficial to the visitor and local person alike. From the headstone inscriptions we often learn not only the name of the deceased but also that of their next of kin, spouse's maiden name, numbers of children, place of residence, and above all, age at death. However, not every family in pre-famine Ireland was in a position to provide an inscribed burial memorial to aid the research of future generations. But those who did unknowingly provided a family record pre-dating the official recording of births, deaths and marriages.

Sarah Tarlow,[3] who did an in-depth study of burial memorials on Orkney, has noted that headstones are 'both deliberately communicative and unintentionally revealing'. By 'deliberately communicative' she meant the inscriptions while 'unintentionally revealing' is in reference to the decoration or iconography. Perhaps her theory is more relevant to a multi-cultural or multi-denominational society. At Kilnahue, based solely on the headstone iconography, it is certain that all burials were Christian. Though this may be expected in 18th century Ireland, the situation in other Christian countries is not as simple. Many contemporary British and North American Christian societies used a disproportionate amount of secular symbolism on their burial memorials. These include urns, hourglasses, willow trees, floral motifs and references to the deceased's trade or profession. But all headstones at Kilnahue display Christian symbolism, a feature common throughout most of Ireland.

It is of course also relevant that some Irish headstones display scarce examples of indigenous folk art. Particularly interesting examples of this art are those stones depicting 'The Symbols of Christ's Passion', a favourite subject of many stone cutters during the latter half of the 18th and continuing into the early years of the 19th centuries. A number of these are signed by the masons involved; others may be

[2] Walton, J.C. 1980. Pictorial Decoration on East Waterford Tombstones. Decies 14, 67-83
[3] Tarlow, Sarah. 1999. Bereavement and Commemoration: an archaeology of mortality. Blackwell Publishers, Oxford.

attributed to a known mason according to style. At Kilnahue there are several examples of the work of those better known stone cutters, Denis Cullen of Monaseed and James Byrne who is known to have lived near Ferns and who later moved to Enniscorthy. Examples of the work of lesser known masons Martin Kenney and Patrick Donnelley are also found there. During the course of the survey the occurrence of an 18th century headstone signed by J. Lee was confirmed. He seems to be un-named in any previously published literature on the subject. There is a late 18th century stone signed by a second D. Cullen, said to be a son or nephew of the first, and also a headstone cut and signed by a John Byrne. Two early 19th century headstones by another mason, D. Toole, were identified during the survey, together with one by Walsh of Carlow and another signed A..N. Enniscorthy. However, by the latter half of the 19th century the individual headstone, made locally to order, had lost popularity. They were often replaced by mass produced examples displaying conventional motifs. These were sometimes imported as blanks and subsequently cut to order. In general, throughout Ireland, the older styles and indigenous art disappeared after the famine years. Late 19th and early 20th century memorials at Kilnahue are by Travers, Nolan, Scally, Cosgrave, Doyle, Grannan and Murphy.

The earliest published interest in Irish burial memorials appeared in the *Journal of the Association for the Preservation of the Memorials of the Dead*, established in 1888. Twelve volumes were produced before the publication ceased in the 1930s. The journal had concentrated on the monuments of the rich and famous and little if anything was added to acknowledge the indigenous folk art found on the ordinary headstones. Possibly during the run of this journal many headstones were considered 'too modern' for inclusion. Although inscription readings were sometimes published in provincial journals during the first half of the 20th century, little attention was paid to headstone decoration. The first serious study of iconography happened in the 1940s when A. K. Longfield published a series of articles in the *Journal of the Royal Society of Antiquaries of Ireland*. In these she addressed the work of the most noticeable and prominent memorial masons working in the south east, mostly in the Wexford, Wicklow and Carlow areas[4]. She also surveyed the work of the un-named Kilsheelan / Kilmurry mason who worked in the South Tipperary / Kilkenny / North Waterford area. In 1998 Eoin Grogan published an article[5] on Denis Cullen's work in *Wicklow Archaeology and History*. He identified eight headstones by Cullen at Kilnahue and also referred to signed stones by James Byrne, Martin Kenney and Patrick Donnelley. During the past number of years the inscriptions at Kilnahue have also been partially recorded[6].

It was never the purpose of this survey to re-trace the steps of those earlier researchers but to try something new. Accordingly a decision was made to include

---

[4] For further reading on this subject see Longfield's contributions to the *Journal of the Royal Society of Antiquaries of Ireland* 1943, 1944, 1945, 1946, 1947, 1948 and 1954.
[5] Grogan, E. 1998. Eighteenth century headstones and the stone mason tradition in County Wiklow: Denis Cullen of Monaseed . In C. Corlette and A. O'Sullivan (eds) *Wicklow Archaeology and History* 1, 41 – 61.
[6] The work of Kathleen Greene and the Explore Group's recording of headstone inscriptions at Kilnahue (2001) is acknowledged. A selection was also recorded by Brian J. Cantwell.

all of the headstones in the churchyard. This encouraged the recording of other iconographic details popular in the locality as well as the spectacular 'Passion Symbol' stones of the great masons. It also allowed the recording of all the inscribed memorials, regardless of age. This helped the tracing of memorial development and changing styles between the mid 18th and mid 20th centuries. However, the iconography or decorative motifs executed by the old headstone cutters had not been fully explored. Previous work in this area had concentrated on the spectacular and had more or less ignored the mundane. Archaeology emphasises the necessity of recording everything including the ordinary in order to obtain as detailed as possible an understanding of past societies. Therefore to record the mundane is just as important as to record the spectacular. Just as today, everybody's taste was not the same; neither could everybody afford the best headstone carvers. Indeed many of those who died in pre-famine Ireland and since, could not afford any headstone. It is also possible that many did not choose to have a headstone due to their society's traditional cultural practice; it often takes a new idea a while to catch on. There are, no doubt, many buried beneath the uninscribed rough grave markers at Kilnahue. It is certain that throughout past centuries there were untold numbers buried there, and throughout Ireland, without any grave marker. During the greater part of Kilnahue's history, it was far more important that the body be buried in consecrated ground within the community in which the person lived, there to rest until the resurrection on the last day.

The Survey

A number of weeks were spent in the classroom addressing the background history of the headstone, associated theory and survey methodology, before proceeding to Kilnahue churchyard and commencing the fieldwork. An archaeological approach was taken, as on an archaeological excavation site. Each 'context', or in this case headstone, was allocated an individual number. A sheet was designed to aid the recording of relevant information (Figure 1). Rubbings were done of most stones, sometimes to help resolve difficult inscriptions and / or decoration, but also to aid off site identification and research (Photographs 2, 3 and 4).

Photographs 2 and 3: Headstone Recording

During the survey there was a consciousness of potential damage to the environment. In the 21st century it comes naturally to most to bring away their water bottles and food wrappers and dispose of them safely. But unfortunately many ancient churchyards and burial memorials throughout Ireland are still being damaged, not only by the deposition of rubbish, but unknowingly by people with the very best of intentions. This survey was conducted without any artificial aids. Headstones are not always easy to record. Some are very weathered; others are covered in lichen or moss. Chemicals should never be used to remove these natural growths. Although their occurrence may obscure some detail, chemical removal may do greater long term damage, not only to the surface of the stone but to the flora and fauna in the vicinity. Due to the nature, location and function of a churchyard, many of them retain scarce and rare examples of native flora, which has often disappeared from the surrounding countryside. Old headstones should not be 'cleaned'. Please remember that future generations may want to see them too!

Photograph 4: Rubbing of Memorial Number 72

If an inscription or iconography is worn, nothing will revive it. Rubbings will enhance the lettering or decoration and the basics can be recorded without recourse to 'cleaning'. Fix suitable paper to the stone with masking tape, then wrap carbon paper around a sponge and rub away. A little practice and you are off. Recording will be better done before noon when the sun is on the eastern face of the stone – wait for a good angle. An elderly gentleman from Carrick-on-Suir, Hugh Ryan, recorded difficult headstone inscriptions at Mothel, Co. Waterford, with the aid of a flashlight in the dark. He did an excellent job. But it's not suggested that everybody should do the same. Headstones are often very difficult to photograph well. Let the sunlight and a bit of patience help; a spray of clean water on the stone may improve the detail.

To publish this work at Kilnahue in book format was not part of the original plan. The idea was to do a more concise survey of the iconography and inscriptions and produce an article suitable for a local historical and archaeological journal. But the survey took on a life of its own. One hundred and twenty six memorials were recorded in total. All of these were not conventionally inscribed but it was considered that the inclusion of some 'rough stones' would enhance the overall result.

Gerry Mullins

Gerry Mullins holds a BA in Archaeology and History and a First Class Honours MA in Archaeology from University College, Cork. He is licensed as an Archaeological Consultant by The Department of the Environment, Heritage and Local Government and as such has directed excavations on several archaeological sites throughout Ireland. He is a member of the Institute of Archaeologists of Ireland and is registered with The Teaching Council as an Archaeology Teacher in the Further Education Sector.

Matty Duggan, Secretary

Headstone Record Sheet

Site Name and #   **Stone #**   **Photograph #**

Stone Geology:	Limestone ☐	Sandstone ☐	Granite ☐	Slate ☐	Other
Dimensions	Height	Width	Thickness Comment:	Regular: Yes ☐	No ☐
INSCRIPTION	Incised ☐	Relief ☐	Legible Yes ☐	No ☐	Partially ☐
Size & Form of Lettering:					
Condition	Poor ☐	Fair ☐	Good ☐	Very Good ☐	Cleaned ☐ Damaged ☐
DECORATION	Incised ☐	Relief ☐	Both ☐	Discernable: Yes ☐ No ☐ Partially ☐	
Condition	Poor ☐	Fair ☐	Good ☐	Very Good ☐	Cleaned ☐ Damaged ☐
Area Decorated:					
Maker's Name	No ☐	Yes ☐ Position			
Erection Date					
Back of Stone	Rough ☐ Smooth ☐ Decorated ☐	Inscribed ☐ Incised ☐ Relief ☐	Condition: Feature:	Poor ☐ Fair ☐ Good ☐ V Good ☐	
Edges:	Square ☐	Rounded ☐	Chamfered ☐	Other	
HEADSTONE	In situ ☐	Relocated ☐	Upright ☐	Leaning ☐	Fallen ☐
Location:	In Church ☐	In Yard ☐	Position		
Orientation:	East/West ☐	Other:			
Burials Recorded: #	Male	Female	Children < 12 years		
Occupation or Symbol:	No ☐	Yes ☐			
Weather Conditions:		General Condition:			
Recorded by:	**Date:**	**Time:**			

Sketch & Inscriptions

Figure 1: Headstone Record Sheets

This publication is intended as both a reference and a guide to the burial memorials at the ancient churchyard of Kilnahue, County Wexford. It is hoped that it will be an aid to the needs of the archaeology, history, or genealogy student, as well as being helpful to the casual churchyard visitor or tourist.

One hundred and twenty six recorded memorials at Kilnahue are easily referenced by number and location. The information contained within includes the inscription, description of the iconography employed on each stone and reference to the mason when known. A photograph of each memorial is also reproduced. Inscribed memorial dates range from 1716 to 1946.

Matt Duggan,
Secretary,
Gorey Churchyard Heritage Group

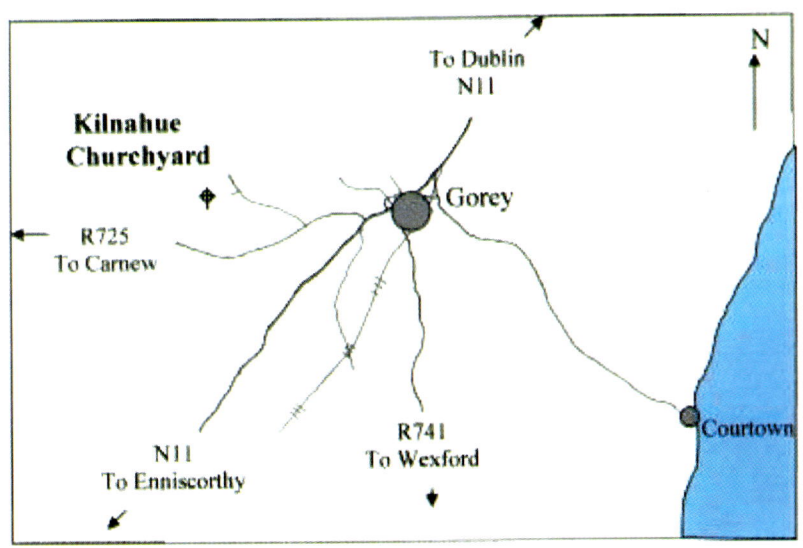

Location Map & Directions

Before heading south on the N11 from Gorey to Enniscorthy turn right for Carnew at the monument. Turn right into Kilnahue Lane at Gorey Educate Together and Gaelscoil. The Churchyard is approximately 1.5 km on the left hand side.

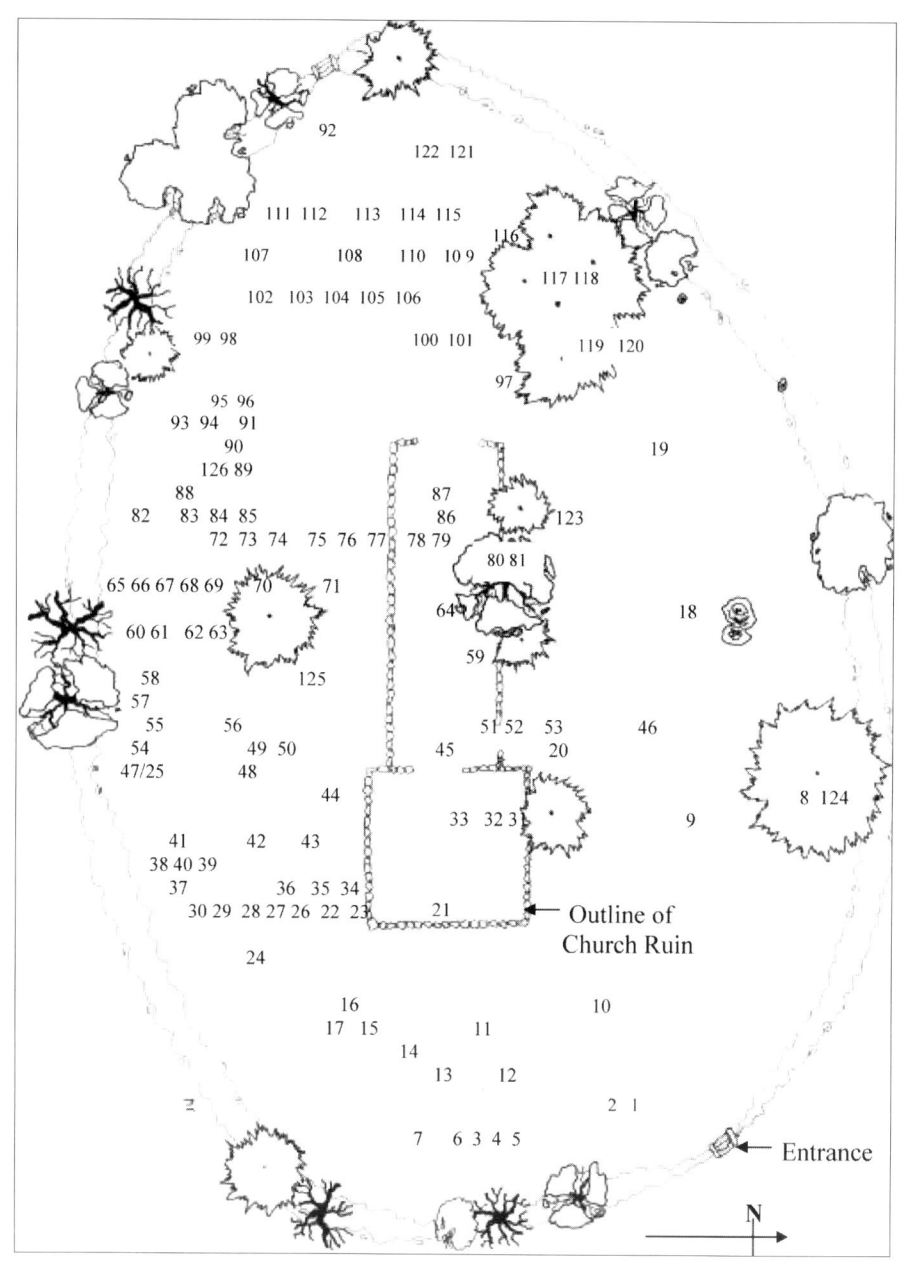

Plan of Kilnahue Churchyard with approximate locations of the surveyed memorials

Darcy 1767 and 1847 Memorial Number 1

This headstone is 122 cm in height by 85 cm in width and is 5 to 6 cm in depth.

The stone is signed beneath the decorative panel on the right by the mason, M. Kenney, Ballylough.

Iconography:

The Darcy headstone portrays the Passion Symbols, the traditional representation of the crucifixion of Jesus. Two fugures in profile flank the cross. These represent Mary, His mother, and Mary Magdalene, who, according to the Gospel accounts, were present. Although both figures are usually depicted with halos, Mary, the mother of Jesus, is often identified as Queen of Heaven by the occurrence of a crown on her head, especially on the better preserved examples. The serpent occurs beneath the cross, which is symbolic of Jesus' victory over evil. The moon crescent and the sun in glory are illustrated in the background. A representation of the temple occurs on the right and the tomb is portrayed on the left. The I H S motif occurs beneath.

The Inscription Reads:

Here lies the Body of Murthew Darcy who dep^d this life Feb 9th 1767 agd 33 Yrs. Also the body of Mickl Darcy who dep^d this life Jan 2nd 1847 age^d 67 yrs. Lord have mercy on their souls is inscribed at the base.

Based on the style of the inscription, there is some doubt regarding the accuracy of the second date. Perhaps the mason intended to inscribe 1784 and confused the order of the numerals.

MD Memorial Number 2

This rough stone is located directly inside the churchyard entrance. It measures approximately 40 cm in height by 43 cm in width and is between 6 and 7 cm in depth. The letters MD are roughly inscribed.

During the course of the survey it was decided to include some of the rough burial markers at Kilnahue as being representative of the 321 undated and unnamed stones on the site. To arrive at this number the site was sectioned using ropes and an accurate count of the rough burial markers was undertaken by Matty Duggan and John Nangle.

These stones date, naturally, from an unknown period, but many may be contemporary with the dated headstones as they are intermingled and are not confined to a specific area. Tradition in parts of the country suggests that it was customary to take a stone from a nearby church ruin to mark a burial. This is quite a reasonable theory, as most medieval burial grounds were associated with church buildings. Also, the stones from the church might have had a spiritual association. It is unlikely that local residents would have taken stone from an old church for any other purpose.

Others have proposed that this practice was started by grave diggers in order to identify vacant ground. Although the tradition has its roots in the period prior to the introduction of the headstone, it probably continued for some time afterwards.

Hobbs 1946 Memorial Number 3

Height:	156 cm
Width:	68 cm
Depth:	7 cm

Iconography:

The Hobbs headstone is typical of the 'Celtic Revivalist' type, displaying the ringed cross. 'Celtic' whorl motifs occupy the cross arms. The Sacred Heart is depicted in the centre. An interlace pattern decorates the neck of the cross shaft.

The manufacturer's name, Murphy, Gorey, is incised at the base of the stone.

The Inscription Reads:

Erected by Margaret Hobbs Inchicore Dublin In loving memory of her husband Thomas Hobbs died 17th Dec 1946 aged 84 yrs.
R.I.P. is incised at the base.

This headstone has fallen and is lying close to the churchyard entrance on the left.

The use of the word 'Celtic' when describing Irish art or sculpture is generally a 19th century invention. It is associated with an emerging sense of national identity and separateness prevalent in nationalist Ireland at the time. The ancient high crosses and their iconography are more correctly described as Irish or Insular sculpture and art.

Hobbs and Kavanagh 1873, 1901 and 1913 Memorial Number 4

Height: 129 cm
Width: 61 cm
Depth: 8 cm

Iconography:
This 'Celtic' cross was erected in the early years of the 20th century and the style is typical of the period. The *Agnus Dei*, or Lamb of God lying on a cross, is used as a central decorative motif. Shamrock, again typical of the 'Celtic Revivalist' period, occurs as ornamentation on the cross arms.

The manufacturer's name, M. Travers, Gorey, is incised in the lower left corner.

The Inscription Reads:
Erected by Mary Hobbs of Gorey in memory of her husband Thomas Hobbs died 13th Nov 1901 aged 74 years. Also her grandson John Kavanagh died 19th May 1901 aged 22 years. Her daughter Mary Anne died 21st of May 1873 aged 13 years. Her children Thomas Michael and James died young. The above Mary Hobbs died 30th Jan 1913 aged 78 years.

Shamrock motifs on an Irish headstone at Kincumber South, New South Wales: the process used, inlaying lead, is similar on the Australian and Kilnahue headstones.

Photograph: John Nangle.

Hobbs 1878, 1879, 1914, 1921 and 1936 Memorial Number 5

Height: 160 cm
Width: 59 cm
Depth: 8 cm

Iconography:

This headstone is typical of those manufactured in the late 19th and early 20th centuries. The memorial is reminiscent of the traditional headstone surmounted by a 'Celtic' style cross. Three small crosses are portrayed at the arm terminals. The Lamb of God is represented lying on a cross as the principal design in the centre.

The manufacturer's name, M. Travers, Gorey, is incised on the lower left corner

The Inscription Reads:

Erected by Michael Hobbs of Gorey in memory of his father Thomas Hobbs died 12th Jan 1878 aged 80 years. His mother Mary Hobbs died 6th June 1879 aged 72 years. His sister Eliza Hobbs died 21st April 1914 aged 79 years. His sister died young. Also the above Michael Hobbs died 9th Sep^t 1921 aged 80 years. His sister Bridget died 10th Sep^t 1936 aged 83 yrs.

The stone is very similar in morphology to the Hobbs / Kavanagh Memorial Number 4 which was also cut by Travers. Both headstones record several burials within a similar date range and perhaps were erected about the same time.

Illegible Memorial Number 6

Height:	62 cm
Width:	38 cm
Depth:	16 cm

Iconography:

This small granite headstone has been severely weathered. Only a faint outline of the crossed I H S motif is detectable on the upper portion of the stone.

The inscription is illegible. However, as the stone is in line with four Hobbs headstones, there is a probability that it belongs to the same family.

There are six granite headstones at Kilnahue, only two of which are currently legible: Conor Number 61, records a burial in 1745 and Byrne Number 113, records burials in 1741 and in 1759. Based on the Byrne inscription, it is apparent that it was erected following the second recorded burial. In common with the Byrne and Conor examples, three of the illegible granite headstones display the I H S Monogram surmounted by a cross. These are Numbers 65, 112 and the above Number 6. There is nothing discernable on the sixth stone, Number 49. However, based on the common I H S motif identified on five of the six granite headstones, and the dating of two, there is no reason to suggest that all are not contemporary and probably date to the mid 18th century.

Hobbs 1818 and 1841 Memorial Number 7

Height: 134 cm
Width: 94 cm
Depth: 10 cm

Unfortunately, the decoration on the Hobbs headstone was lightly carved and is currently difficult to discern.

Iconography:

The principal or central motif consists of the crossed I H S Monogram within a rayed circle. This sits comfortably into an elaborate *gloria* scroll, flanked by *ciboria* set within domed arches. A floral motif decorates the upper portion of the stone.

The Inscription Reads:

Erected by Alexander Hobbs in mem^y of his father Alexander Hobbs who dep^d this life aug 22 nd 1818 aged 50 years. Also his mother Mary Hobbs dep^d dec 11 th 1841 agd 56 yrs

This headstone is very similar in style to that of Connor Number 115, which is signed by J. Nol.n, Ferns, the 'a' of Nolan being missing. Although the Hobbs headstone is unsigned, it possibly came from the same source.

Webb 1868 and 1894 Memorial Number 8

Height:	174 cm
Width:	74 cm
Depth:	10 cm

Iconography:

Again, this is typical of later 19th century memorials, which often incorporate the older type headstone morphology beneath an upper 'Celtic Cross' addition. The Lamb of God is portrayed as a principal motif with shamrock decoration on the arms, continuing the 'Celtic' theme.

Richardson and Scarry[1] noted that there is no certain origin for the ring employed on the ancient crosses, but suggest that it 'demonstrates the tendency of Irish artists always to work within their own idiom'.

This headstone has fallen and now lies on its back in the churchyard.

The headstone manufacturer's name, M. Travers, is inscribed on the lower left.

The Inscription Reads:

Erected by Edward Webb of Gorey in memory of his mother Anne Webb died 30th of October 1868 Aged 50 years. His father John Webb died 26th October 1894 aged 82 years.

In many instances the Kilnahue headstones display the maker's name. The large late 19th and early 20th century stones are more correctly described as manufactured. In the Post-Famine era, the individual vernacular stone cutter had more or less disappeared from the scene. A changing culture demanded a more conventional product. Many of the new types were mass - produced, a development which is more noticeable in the bigger cities. But small rural areas sometimes continued to produce indigenous patterns to order at the request of a client.

---

[1] Richardson, H. and Scarry, J. 1990. *An Introduction to Irish High Crosses*. Mercier Press, Cork. Page 12.

Brazil 1886, 1888 and 1914 Memorial Number 9

Iconography:

This is a 'Celtic' cross type. An intertwined I H S motif was used as the principal decoration.

The Inscription Reads:

In memory of Denis Brazil died Oct 12th 1886 aged 57 his wife Sarah Brazil died April 10th 1888 aged 44 his daughter Julia died August 31 1914 aged 30. On those souls sweet Jesus have mercy

Unfortunately the Brazil memorial has fallen and is currently lying in four separate pieces in the north eastern area of the churchyard. Perhaps the fate of the Brazil headstone illustrates the value of preserving by record, which is after all, the purpose of the survey.

A similar intertwined I H S motif is noted on Murphy Number 94 and on Byrne Number 32. All date from the same general period, perhaps indicating a common source.

Darcy 1820 and 1828 Memorial Number 10

The large Darcy headstone leans forward. Dimensions are 132 cm in height by 94 cm in width and 12 cm in depth

Although the decorative motifs on the Darcy headstone are extremely ornate, the carving was weak and is difficult to discern. The decorated area is large and occupies a 49 cm deep lunette above the inscription.

Iconography:
This is a richly decorated headstone. An altar and tabernacle occur as a central motif, surmounted by two angels beneath a dome. Monstrances, in which the Sacred Host was traditionally displayed, border the central decoration. These motifs are enclosed by a rayed circle. *Ciboria* occur at either side within Gothic panels. A *gloria* scroll opens across the curving top of the headstone.

The Inscription Reads:
Here lieth the remains of John Darcy who Departed this life January 12th 1828 aged 60 years Also his Mother Sarah Darcy who departed this life July 16th 1820 aged 72 years

Bolger 1780 Memorial Number 11

Height: 89 cm
Width: 55 cm
Depth: 5 cm

Iconography:
It is unusual to find this variation in the deployment of the crossed I H S motif. Instead of the usual form, the mason has inscribed I † S without the H. It is possible that the stone cutter did not fully understand the significance of the Monagram and was simply reproducing his perception of what he had seen elsewhere.

The Inscription Reads:
Here lyeth the Body of Edward Bolger who departed this life March[h] the 1st 1780 AG[d] 60 years. Lord Have Mercy on his Soul

The Bolger headstone represents an attractive example of plain Irish indigenous art dating from the latter half of the 18th century.

The stylised capital H occurs on many of the memorials at Kilnahue. Note also the 'w' of the word 'who' and the letter 'p' of the word 'departed'. Neither are correctly formed. The common practice of fitting a word to a line, as was done with 'march', by placing the final 'h' above the 'c' is also noted.

The study of headstone lettering has developed over the past number of years. A recent publication has addressed the subject in some detail[2].

---

[2] Thomson, G. 2009. *Inscribed in Remembrance Gravemarker lettering: form, function and recording.* Wordwell, Dublin.

Nolan and Byrne 1847, 1852, 1865, 1868 and 1873
Memorial Number 12

Height: 188 cm
Width: 78 cm
Depth: 9 cm

The headstone has fallen and is at present lying face upwards in the churchyard.

Iconography:
Decoration on the Nolan / Byrne headstone is not pronounced and occupies only a 25 cm area on the top. It consists of a cross within a plain circle, which is flanked on either side by the crossed I H S motif

The Inscription Reads:

Erected by Judith Nolan Clogue in memory of her son Thomas Nolan who departed this life Septr 15th 1868 aged 23 years Also her father Hugh Byrne of Coleshall who dep^d this life Febuary 25th 1847 aged 85 years. Also her mother Mary Byrne who depd this life 25th May 1852 aged 88 years. Also her brother Patrick Byrne who dep^d this life 6th January 1865 aged 65 years. Heare Also repose the remains of the above name Judith Nolan who dep^d this life 13th December 1873 aged 66 years. Reqiescant in Pace Amen

From the inscription on the Nolan / Byrne memorial, we note the practice of using a burial plot several years before erecting a headstone. In the above instance, 21 years has elapsed between the deaths of Thomas Nolan and his grandfather, Hugh Byrne.

Keoghoe 1774 Memorial Number 13

This stone measured 68 cm in height by 53 cm in width and is 5 cm in depth.

Iconography:

The simple iconography on this headstone consists of the crossed I H S motif within a rayed circle. This is flanked on either side by a cherub. Close examination reveals a checkerboard pattern in the background.

The Inscription Reads:

Here lieth the Body of Patrick Keoghoe Dep^d 9th May 1774 Ag^d 74. Lord have mercy on his Soul

In all cases the non-standard spellings of words and names used on the headstones has been carefully reproduced.

Kvghoe 1772 and 1773 Memorial Number 14

Height: 109 cm
Width: 76 cm
Depth: 9 cm

No decoration is apparent. The stone itself is in generally poor condition. A large flake has come away from the upper right corner. It is not proposed that the headstone's condition has destroyed the decoration: it is most likely that there never was any.

The Inscription Reads:

Here lieth the body of Mary Kvghoe alias (broken at this point) *who dep^d this life 1772 aged 72 yrs Also the body of John Kvghoe who died 1773 aged 17 years Also ye body of Willm Kvaghoe aged 32 years. Lord have mercy on their souls*

This headstone is probably home-made: the inscription is well cut but by an amateur. The spelling of the surname, Kvghoe, replacing the letter 'u' with the letter 'v', was common practice at the time. A capital letter U was generally written as V. This may be noted on the coinage of the period when the Latin version of the king's name was written as 'GEORGIVS'. But the rule was not always adhered to, even in print. The practice was also widespread when using lower case letters, as above.

Cauanach Memorial Number 15

This small stone measures 28 cm in height by 26 cm in width and is 6 cm in depth.

Iconography:

A small cross is incised above the short inscription.

The Inscription Reads:

Here Lyeth Willm Cauanach

Although not exactly a rough uninscribed stone, the memorial to Willm Cauanach seems to be only one step removed. The usual practice of substituting 'v' for 'u' is reversed so that the 'u' has been substituted for 'v'. It is tentatively suggested that the Cauanach headstone, which perhaps should be more correctly referred to as a burial marker, dates from the early 18th century.

Bready 1761 Memorial Number 16

Height:	114 cm
Width:	56 cm
Depth:	9 cm

Some damage has occurred to the left side of the stone.

Iconography:
Ornamentation consists of the I H S motif surmounted by a cross. Decorative spirals occur above.

The Inscription Reads:

Here Lyeth the Body of Margrett Bready Who Departed this Life ye 20 June 1761 Age^d 29 ye^{rs}

Spirals are noted in Irish art from the earliest times. They occur on Neolithic passage tombs of the fourth millennium BC and on the high crosses of the Early Medieval period. It is probable that such art served a spiritual as well as a decorative function[3].

---

[3] For further reading on Neolithic art and the general period read: *Newgrange and the Bend in the Boyne* by Geraldine Stout, published by Cork University Press in 2003, or *Irish Megalithic Tombs* by Elizabeth Shee Twohig, published in 1990 by Shire Archaeology.

Boulger and Cullen 1770, 1847 and 1855 Memorial Number 17

Height:	134 cm
Width:	65 cm
Depth:	8 cm

Most of Denis Cullen's passion headstones have a common theme: the crucified Christ, centurion on horseback and one or two soldiers and/or angels.

Iconography:

The Boulger memorial portrays the crucified Christ as a central motif. A mounted centurion, dressed in 18th century military uniform and holding a musket, occurs on the right. Between the horse's head and the cross, a weathered figure may be observed. She is wearing a crown, which identifies her as Mary the mother of Jesus and Queen of Heaven. On the left, a soldier holding a lance is piercing Jesus' side. Two angels, one of whom is seated playing a harp, occur behind him. A peacock, representing the resurrection, occurs left of the seated angel. Four winged cherubs float above the scene. Other symbols depicted include the moon crescent in the lower right corner and the sun in glory in the left. The I H S Monogram is set beneath the cross.

Although this stone is not signed, it is cut in the style of Denis Cullen of Monaseed.

The Inscription Reads:

Here Lyeth the Body of Elinor Boulger Who departed this Life the 6th Day of January 1770 AGd 56 years. Lord have Mercy on her Soul Amen. Martin Cullen of Gorey died 11th April 1855 Aged 63 Years. His wife Bridget died 4th Feb 1847 Aged 53 years

Differences in lettering styles between the 18th and 19th century inscriptions are very obvious on this headstone.

Fitzsimons and Fitzgerald 1845 and 1888 Memorial Number 18

Height: 190 cm
Width: 80 cm
Depth: 10 cm

Iconography:
A stylized I H S motif in Gothic script occurs at the cross arm intersection. This is the only decoration on the headstone.

The manufacturer's name, Travers, Gorey, is inscribed in italics at the base.

The Inscription Reads:
Erected by Her Son James in memory of Sarah Fitzsimons of Creagh who depd this life 18 th Oct 1888 Aged 75 years. Her two Daughters Barbara & Mary Anne who died Young. Her Sister Margaret Fitzgerald died 5 th Sept 1845 Aged 22 Years. R.I.P.

Prior to modern thinking and tradition, children were rarely mentioned by name on headstones. There are several examples at Kilnahue inscribed with the phrase 'children who died young'. This is also a reminder that medical knowledge was less advanced than today and that unfortunately many children died young.

Uninscribed Memorial Number 19

This rough sub-triangular sandstone bears no inscription but a probable rough cross has been incised on its face. It measures approximately 35 cm by 35 cm. As stated, a number of these small rough stones have been included in the survey in order to present a representative sample of the burial memorials at Kilnahue.

It may be noted that the oldest burials occur east, west and south of the church ruins. These were the choice places of burial, as it was believed throughout the centuries that the northern side was not as 'holy'. There are many rough stones occupying the northern side of the church at Kilnahue, and indeed of other medieval church ruins throughout Ireland. Among the various social groups that may be buried in the northern area are those who did not have traditional rights in the churchyard. This area may also have been reserved for strangers who died when passing through the locality.

Modern burial grounds, including those attached to the newly built 19th century churches, seem not to have continued this tradition, particularly in urban areas. Perhaps the reason was largely practical, due to the unavailability of space.

Byrne 1890 and 1892 Memorial Number 20

The headstone has fallen and is currently lying on its back. Measurements were 186 cm in length, 79 cm in width and 10 cm in depth.

The manufacturer's name, Travers, Gorey, is inscribed at the base.

Iconography:
A 'Celtic Revivalist' style cross. The central motif features the Lamb of God, or *Agnus Dei*. Stylized shamrock decoration occurs on each of the cross arms, in keeping with the 'Celtic' theme.

The Inscription Reads:
Erected by his children in memory of their Father Patrick Byrne of Gorey Who died 5th Feb 1890 Aged 68 Years. His Son William died 16th Nov 1892 Aged 14 Years. Also his four children who died young. R.I.P

Byrne 1879, 1886, 1892 and 1898 Memorial Number 21

Height:	165 cm
Width:	66 cm
Depth:	10 cm

Iconography:

This 'Celtic' cross is very similar to other examples at Kilnahue. Note the openwork ring with the Lamb of God lying on a cross deployed as the principle central motif. Four stylized crosses occupy the arms. This Byrne memorial is in particularly good condition, allowing the viewer to appreciate the skill of the maker.

This memorial is located within the ruins of the church at Kilnahue.

The manufacturer's name, M. Travers, Gorey, is incised at the headstone base.

The Inscription Reads:

Erected by William Byrne of Gorey Hill in memory of his wife Anastatia Byrne who died 4th of August 1879 aged 56 years. Also his two children who died young. His son Silvester died 6th of August 1886 aged 20 years. His son Thomas died 1st Dec 1892 aged 43 years. Also the above William Byrne died 29th Nov 1898 aged 72 years.

Mordin 1763 Memorial Number 22

Height: 116 cm
Width: 58 cm
Depth: 6 cm

Unfortunately this example of Cullen's work is splitting and the iconography is in danger of being lost.

The Iconography:

An I H S motif surmounted by a large cross fills the lunette above the inscription. This headstone has been attributed to Cullen by Longfield[4] and Grogan[5], based on the style and quality of the carving.

The Inscription Reads:

Here lyeth the body of Ann Mordin Who Departed ye 22nd June 1763 AGd 26 ys All so Catharine Mordin died ye 15th December 1766 AG 58

This is the only headstone at Kilnahue attributed to the mason Denis Cullen of Monaseed that does not display his standard crucifixion scene. He was among the greatest Irish vernacular sculptors of his generation. Cullen had worked as a quarry man and it is probable that, apart from his figure carving and artistic abilities, he was excellent at choosing the right piece of stone. Much of his work is still fresh and most of the stones are in good condition after almost 250 years. However, on this occasion he seems to have been in error with his stone choice.

---

[4] Longfield, A. 1943. Some Eighteenth Century Irish Tombstones. *The Journal of the Royal Society of Antiquaries of Ireland* 73, 28 – 39.
[5] Grogan, E. 1998. Eighteenth century headstones and the stone mason tradition in County Wicklow: the work of Dennis Cullen of Monaseed. In: C. Corlett and A. O'Sullivan (eds) *Wicklow Archaeology and History* 1, 41 – 61.

This sandstone example is preserved to a height of 51 cm and is about the same width. It measured 5 cm in depth.

The Preserved Inscription Reads:

Ag.....Years. Lord have mercy on hr Soul Amen.

There was no evidence for the upper fragment of this stone on the site. The word 'her' is obviously spelled 'hr'.

The majority of the headstones at Kilnahue are of sandstone. Although this is a very suitable medium for carving, it splits very easily, as it has a layered structural formation. It is likely that an experienced quarry man or mason choose his stone very carefully, but could not control the effects of time. Although there was no evidence at Kilnahue of any upper headstone fragments lying about, a destroyed fragment would quickly become overgrown and sink beneath the sod in a relatively short time.

Murphy 1784 Memorial Number 24

Height:	91 cm
Width:	57 cm
Depth:	5 cm

Iconography:

Detail on this Murphy headstone is very simple and clear.

The crossed I H S Monogram is set within a rayed circle flanked by winged cherubs.

The Inscription Reads:

Here Lieth the body of Maurice Murphy Dep[d] 10th Oct 1784 Age[d] 45 years. the Lord have mercy on his soul

It was noted that the 's' of 'his' was inscribed backwards.

Cherubs are occasionally used as ornamentation on Irish headstones but rarely reached the popularity or sophistication of design noted in Britain and America. Surveys undertaken in the Massachusetts area of the United States proved the cherub, together with death's heads and willow trees, to be among the three most popular principal decorative motifs employed on early headstones in the region[6].

---

[6] Dethlefsen, E. and Deetz, J. 1966. Death's Heads, Cherubs and Willow Trees: experimental archaeology in colonial cemeteries. *American Antiquity* 31 (4), 502 – 10.

R.I.P. Memorial Number 25

Height:	70cm
Width:	48cm
Depth:	2 – 3 cm

This broken purple slate is located immediately behind the headstone of Edward Darcy, Monument Number 47. It is not fixed and seems to be just lying there loosely. There is no other decoration or inscription apart from the Greek cross and the letters R.I.P.

Had this stone been elsewhere, it may conceivably have been used as a footstone. But there seems to be no tradition of this practice in the area. Such stones were sometimes used to mark the eastern extent of a burial plot, as the headstone was always set on the western end.

It has been traditional since the Late Iron Age for at least some Irish burials to be orientated in a west east direction i.e. with the head towards the west[7]. This was a Roman practice and was introduced through Britain to Ireland about the first century AD. The practice was later adopted by the church and given a Christian significance. Burial markers, when first introduced, were placed at the head, with the result that later headstone inscriptions and decorative motifs faced east. It may be sometimes noted in older churchyards that a headstone faces west. If so, it is likely to belong to a parish priest, as the orientation of the burial enabled him to rise facing his congregation on Judgment Day. But there instances when headstones have been re-set and incorrectly orientated.

---

[7] Mullins, Gerry. 2007. Pagan or Christian? Excavation of a hilltop cemetery at Cross, Co. Galway. In Jerry O'Sullivan and Michael Stanley (eds) *New Routes to the Past*. NRA, Dublin. pp 101 – 110.

Murphy 1786 Memorial Number 26

Measurements are 90 cm in height by 86 cm in width by 5 cm in depth

Iconography:

The headstone of John Murphy is well cut, symmetric and clear. An I H S Monogram surmounted by a cross is set above a heart and occurs within a rayed circle. The temple and tomb are set at either side. Headstones of this period often represent the temple as a contemporary church. But this un-named mason seemingly knew his eastern architecture and art. Both temple and tomb structures are represented as being very similar to many eastern mosques or tombs, including the Taj Mahal. Likewise, his portrayal of the date palms flanking the structure are realistic, and in fact are very similar to that species of tree as they appear in early Egyptian and Minoan art. Perhaps we underestimate the training and education of these 18th century rural stone cutters. It is also possible that this particular mason had travelled in the east and had seen the sites first hand, or perhaps he had access to illustrations. Alternatively the client may have travelled and conveyed his wishes to the mason before death.

The Inscription Reads:

Here lies the body of John Murphy who Dep^d this life Sept 29th 1786 AG^D 55. Lord have mercy on his soul

Murphy 1792 Memorial Number 27

Measurements of the Murphy 1792 headstone are 92 cm in height by 79 cm in width and 5 cm in depth.

This headstone is signed by the mason, J. Byrne on the left beneath the decoration.

Iconography:

The iconography employed represents the crucifixion scene with the I N R I displayed above Christ. The serpent and death's head occur at the foot of the cross, symbolic of His victory over evil and death. The two female figures flanking the cross represent Mary, His mother, crowned as Queen of Heaven, and Mary Magdalene. Both of these women, according to the Gospels, were present at the crucifixion. The sun, incorporating a human face, appears behind the figure of Mary. During the medieval period this symbol represented 'Glory'. The structure on the right represents either the temple or the tomb. A palm tree fits nicely in the opposite corner. Arrowhead and I H S motifs decorate the border.

The Inscription Reads:

Here lies the body of Thomas Murphy who dep^d this life Sept 17th 1792 Ag^d 60 yrs. Lord have Mercy on his Soul

Toole 1770 Memorial Number 28

Measurements are 75 cm in height by 64 cm in width and 7 cm in depth.

This headstone is unsigned but is attributed to Cullen based on style.

Iconography:
The crucifixion scene is represented with the mounted centurion on the right. A soldier bearing the lance is portrayed on the left in the act of piercing Jesus' side, as is related in the Gospel accounts. Cullen has dressed the soldiers in 18th century military uniform. The temple, represented as a contemporary church with its steeple, is set in the extreme left. An I H S motif occurs beneath the cross.

The Inscription Reads:
Here Ly the body of John Toole Who Departed this Life 24th January 1770 ag[d] 74 years. Lord have mercy on his soul.

The moulding on top of this headstone is particularly attractive and well-cut. This is a common feature of much of Cullen's work.

Cullin and Daneley 1814 and 1815 Memorial Number 29

Height:	126 cm
Width:	83 cm
Depth:	9 cm

Iconography:

The details on this large Cullin headstone are weak and were only identified through rubbings. The central figure of the crucified Christ is framed within a domed portico, which may represent an altar or tabernacle. A crossed I H S motif, flanked by two angels, is set within the overhead dome. A monstrance occurs on either side of the central decorations. Both display the I H S. These are in turn flanked by *ciboria*.

The Inscription Reads:

Erected by James Cullin in memory of his wife Winford Cullin alias Daneley who Dp this life Jan the 28th 1814 agd 52 and also the body of Patrick Cullin his son who dp this life March the 8th 1815 agd 27.

The *ciboria* as decoration on Irish headstones may have an origin in the depiction of the hourglass on English examples. Reference to Burgess' book[8] will testify to the popularity of the motif in that country. Although the hourglass is sometimes portrayed on Irish headstones, it was never in widespread use. Both symbols have a common morphology, and are easily substituted for each other. It seems that the Irish preferred religious rather than secular motifs to be depicted on their headstones. Archaeological theorists, Hodder and Orton,[9] have suggested that components of one culture may be found 'as components in other cultural assemblages in neighbouring areas'. The Irish use of the *ciborium* in a space formally reserved for the hourglass may be a good example of this.

---

[8] Burgess, F. 1963. *English Churchyard Memorials.* Lutterworth Press, London. Page 168.
[9] Hodder, I. and Orton, C. 1976. *Spacial Analysis in Archaeology.* Cambridge University Press. Page 199

Mooran 1789 and 1804 Memorial Number 30

Height:	140 cm
Width:	77 cm
Depth:	8 cm

Iconography:

The Mooran headstone depicts the I H S motif beneath a large cross within a rayed circle.

The stone is particularly well cut with a checkerboard pattern surrounding the central decoration and covering the lunette area.

This headstone is signed by the mason, W. Lee in the centre beneath the decoration.

The Inscription Reads:

Here Lieth the body of Mary Mooran wh[o] dep[d] this life August the 8th 1789 AG[d] 25 years. Also the Body of Hir father Miles Mooran who dep[d] this life Oct[br] 18th 1804 ag[d] 75 Y[rs]. Lord have Mercy on their Souls Amen.

During the course of her pioneering work in the 1940s, Ada Longfield rediscovered many previously forgotten headstone cutters who worked in the south east of Ireland during the 18th and early 19th centuries. These were published in the *Journal of the Royal Society of Antiquarians of Ireland* between 1943 and 1948, and again in 1954. But the name W. Lee was not recorded. It is nice to know that there may be still unrecorded stone masons out there awaiting discovery.

Sheridan / Byrne 1862, 1866, 1873 and 1902
Memorial Number 31

Height:	177 cm
Width:	77 cm
Depth:	10 cm

This stone is currently leaning forward against the red brick grotto.

Iconography:

The Lamb of God, depicted lying on a cross, is again used on this 'Celtic Revivalist' memorial as a central motif. Shamrock motifs were used to decorate the cross arms.

The manufacturer's name, M. Travers, Gorey, is located in the lower left corner.

The Inscription Reads:

Erected by Mary Sheridan Gorey Hill in memory of her Father Thomas Byrne died 22nd July 1866 aged 78 years. Also her mother Mary Byrne died 10th May 1873 aged 83 years. Also her sister Annie Byrne died 12th June 1862 aged 35 years. Also the above Mary Sheridan died 24th May 1902 aged 76 years. R.I.P.

It is generally considered that the introduction of the 'Celtic' cross as a burial memorial followed an exhibition in Dublin in 1853, organised by the Royal Dublin Society. Italian sculptors had been invited to Ireland to reproduce plaster casts of the original Early Medieval Irish high crosses, which were exhibited to general public acclaim.

An exhibition of those same plaster casts is currently on view at Collins Barracks.

Byrne 1906, 1914 and 1919 Memorial Number 32

Height:	158 cm
Width:	64 cm
Depth:	8 cm

Iconography:

The iconography on the Byrne memorial consists of an intertwined I H S motif in a plain circle.

This white marble memorial is located within the church ruins.

The manufacturer's name, Travers, Gorey, is inscribed in the lower left corner.

The Inscription Reads:

Erected by John Byrne of Creagh in memory of his wife Margaret Byrne who died 28th Feb1906 aged 29 years. Also his five infants. Also his father John Byrne died 7th Dec 1914 aged 86 yrs. Also his mother Mary Anne Byrne died 30th Nov 1919 aged 80 yrs.

The I H S Monogram on the above Byrne headstone is similar to that depicted on the Brazil Number 9 stone. It is also similar to the I H S on the memorial to Denis Murphy Number 94. Perhaps this indicates that all three headstones are by the same manufacturer.

This sandstone memorial is leaning forward and is partially buried. It measures 67 cm in height by 58 cm wide and is 8 cm in depth. The headstone is located within the church ruin.

Iconography:

The unknown mason who carved the headstone of Elizabeth Kinceley used the traditional crossed I H S Monogram within a rayed circle as the principal motif. He then took two of the commonly used passion symbols, the ladder and the pincers holding a nail, to fill the space in the remainder of the lunette.

The Inscription Reads:

Here Lieth the Body of Elizabeth Kinceley Dep^d this Life January 3^d 1779 AG^d 25 Lord have Mercy on her Soul

Measurements are 97 cm in height, 85 cm in width and 6 cm in depth. The headstone is leaning slightly forward.

This headstone is signed beneath the iconography by the mason Martin Kenney.

Iconography:

The Bulger / Dunn headstone is in an excellent state of preservation, although some damage has occurred to the moulding along the top. The crucifixion scene accompanied by Mary the mother of Jesus and Mary Magdalene occurs as the principal motif. The serpent and death's head are portrayed beneath Jesus' feet, symbolizing his sacrificial victory. *Ciboria*, in which the Sacred Host was held, flank the scene. The moon crescent, with its usual human face, and the sun in glory are set on either side. An I H S and arrowhead motifs decorate the border between the iconography and inscription.

The Inscription Reads:

Here lies the Body of Ann Bulger alais Dunn who dep^d this life May 4th 1794 agd 44 Years.

The Dunn headstone measures 97 cm in height by 85 cm in width by 5 cm in depth and is leaning slightly forward and to the left.

This headstone is signed by the mason, J. Byrne, beneath the decoration on the right.

Iconography:
The crucifixion scene is again central to the decorative motifs employed on the Dunn headstone. The serpent and death's head are set beneath the feet of Christ. Mary and Mary Magdalene are portrayed at either side of the cross. A large moon crescent and sun in glory flank these figures. An unusual decorative diamond pattern and I H S Monogram form the border between the iconography and the inscription.

The Inscription Reads:
Here lies the Body of Brien Dunn who Dep^d this life March 25th 1768 Ag^d 48 Y^{rs} Also his wife Margaret Dun^n March 15th 1789 Ag^d 64 Y^{rs} Also his son Miles Dunn July 24th 1798 Ag^d 34 Y^{rs} Also Dennis Dunn his son Sepr 29th 1807 Agd 54 Years. Lord (nothing else is legible)

This is the only recorded burial at Kilnahue during the summer of 1798.

Tighe 1810 and 1826 Memorial Number 36

Height:	94 cm
Width:	71 cm
Depth:	6 cm

The Tighe headstone is in extremely poor condition.

Iconography:
Only a centrally located crossed I H S motif was noted above the inscription. Traces of decoration occur in other areas of the lunette but are not discernable.

The Inscription Reads:

Here lieth the body Timothy Tighe who dep[d] this life Nov 1810 and also his son Andrew Tighe dep 1826 Aged 28 years. Erected by John Tighe. Reqiescant in Pace.

Reading the above inscription is reminiscent of Grogan's study[10] of Denis Cullen's client group. Having discovered that there is a gender imbalance recorded on Cullen's headstones, he continued to further test this observation by surveying memorials by other known masons in a selection of churchyards. The results were similar: there are more male recorded burials than female.

---

[10] Grogan, E. 1998. Eighteenth century headstones and the stone mason tradition in County Wicklow: the work of Denis Cullen of Monaseed. In C.Corlett and A. O'Sullivan (eds) *Wicklow Archaeology and History* 1, 41 – 61.

Redmond 1791 and 1834 Memorial Number 37

Height:	137 cm
Width:	82 cm
Depth:	6 cm

Iconography:

This passion symbol headstone portrays the central figure of the crucified Christ. The serpent and death's head are displayed beneath His feet, as was customary. On the left is Mary, identified by her crown as Queen of Heaven. Beside Mary are the tomb and a tree. A soldier, in 18th century uniform, stands to the right holding a pistol. Further right, a large structure represents the temple. This depiction is very similar to Kenney's temple on Monument Number 1. A disproportionate ladder is set beside the structure. The sun in glory and the moon crescent flank the arms of the crucifix.

This stone is signed by the mason, J. Byrne, in the border area on the right.

The Inscription Reads:

Here lies the Body of Bartholomew Redmond who Dep[d] this life June 21st 1791 Ag[d] 76 Y[rs]. Lord have Mercy on his Soul. Here also lie the Mortal Remains of his Son Moses Redmond of Ballygarrett Deceased March 27th AD 1834 Aged 81 Years. His name is inscribed as a mark of love and esteem by his grateful nephew John Byrne.

During the 18th century headstone inscriptions were rarely personal. It was usual to state the deceased's name, age and date of death. The Redmond example allows an insight into a changing tradition as the 19th century progressed. The emergence of more personal inscriptions is noted.

Byrne, the mason, seems to adopt Cullen's convention of including a soldier in the scene, a theme which he also portrayed on the Richmond Memorial Number 123. Both of these headstones might represent his early work.

Kinslough 1791 Memorial Number 38

Height:	121 cm
Width:	76 cm
Depth:	6 cm

Iconography:

The Kinslough headstone portrays the passion scene. The crucified Christ, as was traditional, is centrally located. Mary, His mother, and Mary Magdalene flank the cross. The tomb occurs on the left and the temple on the right. Both are set within panels. In common with Cullen's depiction of the temple, Kenney represents it as a contemporary church complete with a cross on the steeple.

The headstone is signed by the mason, M. Kenney, beneath the decoration on the left.

The Inscription Reads:

Here lies the Body of Martin Kinslough who Dep^d this life April 12th 1791 Ag^d 88 Y^{rs} Lord have Mercy on his Soul

Although many the masons who worked in the south east during the late 18th and early 19th centuries repeat the same scene, sometimes there is a little variety. At Kilnahue this headstone by Kenney is the only example on the site to illustrate the temple and the tomb within panels on each side of the centrally placed crucifixion.

Unlike many of Cullen's headstones, this representation of the passion scene by Kenney is weak and weathered.

The small Connor headstone measures 50 cm in height by 32 cm in width and is 7 cm in depth.

Iconography:

This is a very simple rectangular headstone displaying just the name of the deceased and the date of death.   An I † S motif is used, rather than the conventional I H S.

The Inscription Reads:

James Connor Departed this life June The 4th 1769 Aged 44 Years

The simplicity of the design suggests that it is contemporary with the inscribed date. In common with Bolger Memorial Number 11, the mason has not used the letter 'H' in the Monogram. Close inspection of the letter 'I' indicates a probable abandoned attempt to form a cross. The mason obviously did not understand the significance of the motif. This is strange, as several headstones depicting the I H S in its proper format had already been erected in the churchyard.

Uninscribed Iron Memorial Number 40

Height:	95 cm
Width:	58 cm
Depth:	2 cm

There is no apparent inscription or maker's name on the cross. It stands set in a stepped concrete plinth, measuring 48 cm by 32 cm at the base.

This 'Celtic' cross is made of forged iron, and is more than likely to have been locally manufactured. It is probable, in common with the numerous stone 'Celtic' crosses at Kilnahue that the three iron crosses, Monuments Number 93 and 111, as well as the above Number 40, date from the late 19th or early 20th centuries.

The Heydon headstone measures 73 cm in height by 66 cm in width and is 12 cm in depth. This is one of the few older limestone monuments on the site.

Iconography:

Iconography on the Heydon headstone consists of the I H S motif surmounted by a cross, flanked by disk decoration.

The Inscription Reads in Capitals:

HERE LIETH THE BODY OF THOMAS HEYDON WHO DEPARTED THIS LIFE OCTOBER THE 6TH 1716 AGED 8 YEARS AND THE BODY OF HONORA HEYDON DECEASED FEBURAY 11TH 1742 AGED 18 YEARS

The Heydon headstone is a good example of a monument being erected decades after a burial. The earliest death recorded, that of Thomas Heydon, was in 1716. But based on headstone style and lettering, it is unlikely that the stone was erected until shortly before the second burial in 1742, which is inscribed in a different script and was obviously added at a later date. The inscription is a scarce example of a named child's burial during this period. It also records the earliest death at Kilnahue.

Redmond 1764 Memorial Number 42

Height:	93 cm
Width:	55 cm
Depth:	9 cm

The condition of the inscription and decoration is poor but the stone is instantly recognizable from its unique shape in the churchyard. It is also, together with Memorial Numbers 41 and 62, one of the three older limestone monuments at Kilnahue.

Iconography:

The principal motif employed was the I H S surmounted by a cross. There was no evidence identified for secondary decoration.

The Inscription Reads:

Here lyeth Ye body of Terince Redmond who departed this life March ye 29th 1764 Aged 72 years. Requiscant in Pace Amen

The Redmond headstone is an unusual shape, displaying a proportionally small lunette and sloping shoulders. There is a small socket set into the top. The reason for this is unknown but it may have been used to hold a small metal or wooden cross.

The above inscribed Terince Redmond lived most of his life during the period of the Penal Laws. Being born, according to the headstone, in 1692, the year after the Jacobite defeat and 'The Flight of the Wild Geese', his early childhood witnessed the introduction of several legal obstructions to property ownership and entry into various professions. Although some were never strictly enforced, the first official discussions concerning the relaxations of these laws began only two years after his death.

Sinnott and Davis 1818 and 1843 Memorial Number 43

The stone stands 127 cm in height by 87 cm in width and is 9 cm in depth.

The stone is signed by the mason, D. Toole, beneath the decoration on the left.

Iconography:
A crossed I H S motif above a small heart occurs within a rayed circle. This is the only iconographic detail on the large Sinnott headstone.

The Inscription Reads:
Erected by M^{RS} Elenor Sinnott of Bishop St Dublin in Memory of her Husband Arthur Sinnott who Dep^d this life the 8th of Feb 1818 agd 38 Y^{rs}. She is left behind in a world of sorrow to deplore the loss of a kind and affectionate husband. He was a tender father, a faithful friend, lived respected, died regretted. Also the son of Michael Sinnott ag^d 3 Y^{rs} and her brother Michael Davis departed this life 8th of April 1843 aged 38 years.

The approach of the above inscription is unique at Kilnahue. First of all the named widow is referred to as 'Mrs', and secondly the inscription continues to eulogize the deceased husband. The Latin phrase *'Memonte Mori'* (A reminder of death) flanks the base of the decorative area.

It is also notable that a deceased child remained un-named, and was identified only by the name of his father.

Byrne 1814 Memorial Number 44

Height:	145 cm
Width:	87 cm
Depth:	6 cm

Although the inscription on this Byrne headstone is easily read, the decoration within the lunette is, in common with most memorials displaying the Altar / Tabernacle scenes, in extremely poor condition.

Iconography:

A cross within a double portico constitutes the central motif. It is not clear if the crucified figure occurs. Monstrances flank the portico. It is probable that the mason represented an altar or tabernacle, a popular decorative theme during the period.

The Inscription Reads:

Here Lieth the Body of Bryan Byrne of B^l Clash C^o Wicklow who depar^t this life Feby. Y 28th 1814 Aged 23 years.

Requieseant in Pace

Sometimes the phrases 'May they / he / she rest in peace', or 'May the Lord have mercy on their / his / her Soul', may be noted following headstone inscriptions. It is often interesting to note the number of burials inscribed, for at times there is a contradiction. A similar inconstancy sometimes occurs with the Latin singular *Requiescat*. The plural *Requiescant*, though misspelled above, occurs on a single recorded burial.

Keating and Kavanagh 1807 and 1808 Memorial Number 45

Height:	139 cm
Width:	81 cm
Depth:	10 cm

There is some damage to the upper right hand corner of the stone.

Iconography:

The decorative motif employed on the Keating headstone portrays the traditional I H S motif surmounted by a cross within a rayed circle. It extends 40 cm from the top. There was no other decoration noted.

The Keating headstone is located within the old church ruin.

The Inscription Reads:

This Stone was Erected by Redmond Keating in Memory of his Father Redmond Keating who Died the 7th of Feb 1807 Aged 79 Y^{rs} also his Mother Mary Keating otherwise Kavanagh who died the 2nd of March 1808 aged 75 yrs. Lord have mercy on their Souls.

Throughout the country, burials are commonly located within old church ruins. The tradition of burying the dead within churches is ancient and was widespread among the European aristocracy, clergy and the better-off in society. Following the Reformation, there were many attempts to ban the practice on the grounds of both theology and hygiene, particularly in Scotland. However, this was not easily done, as intramural burials were lucrative to the church authorities. From the 16th century onwards, many Irish rural parish churches were abandoned or decayed due to neglect. Burials continued within the ruins, partially due to lack of space in the churchyards. But there is no doubt that the inside of the church was considered a primary plot and probably continued to attract higher burial fees for the authorities.

Darcy and Flusk 1827, 1829 and 1850 Memorial Number 46

Height is 150 cm, width is 95 cm and the headstone in 10 cm in depth.

Iconography:

Iconography on the Darcy / Flusk headstone portrays a large cross set within a rayed circle. A small I H S Monogram occurs at the cross arms intersection. Decorative *ciboria* in domed panels flank the central ornamentation.

The Inscription Reads:

Erected by Catherine Darcy of Gowrey in memory of her husband Edward Darcy who departed this life the 10th of February 1850 Aged 48 years Also her Mother Catherine Flusk who dep[d] this life the 26th of January 1827 Aged 65 yrs Also her Father Bryan Flusk who dep[d] this life the 13th of Janry 1829 aged 82 yrs.

Although the traditional format of the I H S motif was never entirely abandoned, changes in style are often noted during the Post Famine period. In this instance the cross has become more prominent and the I H S relegated to a secondary feature.

Darcey 1809 Memorial Number 47

Height is 91 cm, width is 55 cm and depth is 9 cm.

Iconography:

In common with other stones displaying the altar / tabernacle motif, the condition of the iconography is extremely poor. However, the decorative features were identified from rubbings. The crucified figure of Christ is displayed centrally within an ornate portico beneath a crossed I H S Monogram. This scene is flanked by monstrances and *ciboria*. The display is reminiscent of a church altar or tabernacle.

The Inscription Reads:

Here lieth the Body of Edwd Darcey who dep^d this life mar^h 29th 1809 ag^d 58 years. Lord have mercy on his soul

The Department of the Environment, Heritage and Local Government's publication, *An Introduction to the Architectural Heritage of County Wexford*, pictures a headstone at Ferns damaged by gunshot. There are several stones at Kilnahue displaying small holes. But as the above stone is naturally splitting, it seems more likely that a metal bar and molten lead was inserted at some stage to prevent further deterioration of the stone.

Laughlin 1757 and 1788 Memorial Number 48

The Laughlin headstone measures 94 cm in height by 61 cm in width and is 9 cm in depth.

This headstone is not signed but is attributed to Cullen based on its iconography and style.

Iconography:

This is a particularly fine example of Cullen's plainer work, portraying the central figure of Christ on the cross beneath the I N R I. The mounted centurion occurs on the right and the lance bearer on the left in the act of piercing Jesus' side. An I H S Monogram set between two decorative checkerboard panels separate the iconography from the inscription.

The Inscription Reads:

Here Lieth the Body of Darby Laughlin Died 3rd March 1757 AG D 61 years Also patrick Laughlin Died Decemb 16th 1788 AG D 54 years Lord Have mercy on their souls Amen

This is one of the earliest dated headstones attributed to Cullen. The first recorded burial in 1757 probably pre-dates the stone by a number of years.

Illegible Memorial Number 49

The stone is 74 cm in height by 56 cm in width and is 12 cm in depth.

A faint line is discernable extending across the face of the stone 26 cm from the top. It is probable that some iconography occurred above this and that the inscription, as usual, occurred below.

In common with four of the six granite headstones at Kilnahue, this stone is very weathered and there is no indication of an inscription or of any decorative motifs. Two of the granite headstones are legible and both record mid 18th century burials. Five of the stones, including the two legible examples, portray the I H S motif. Based on the available information it is probable that all six are contemporary. Granite is an extremely difficult stone to work with and was perhaps abandoned as a medium by later masons. It is also possible that a convenient sandstone quarry became available.

Aylward 1782 Memorial Number 50

Measurements are 111 cm in height by 96 cm in width by 9 cm in depth.

Iconography:
A large crossed I H S motif occurs above a small heart within a rayed circle.

The Inscription Reads:
Here Lyeth the Body of Sarah Aylward who departed this life the 8th of April 1782 aged 74 years. Lord have mercy on her soul Amen

All of the memorials at Kilnahue display motifs with some religious association. The same may be said of the vast majority of headstones throughout Ireland. In this respect Ireland contrasts greatly with neighbouring England, where headstone ornamentation tends to be more secular. Burgess[11], in his book, *English Churchyard Memorials*, refers to a clergyman in Bristol complaining about the lack of 'Christian Art' in churchyards in 1847.

Although religious affiliations may partially account for the variations in subject matter, it is probable that differences in attitude between industrial and rural societies is also reflected.

---

[11] Burgess quotes from *Remarks on Christian Gravestones,* published by Eccles Carter, Canon of Bristol, in 1847. Page 5

Doyle 1821 Memorial Number 51

Height: 138 cm
Width: 80 cm
Depth: 8 cm

Iconography:

Ornamentation on the Doyle headstone is very worn and difficult to recognize. It seems to be a variant of that identified on other Altar / Tabernacle stones.

A large monstrance occurs as a central motif, framed within a portico composed of four pillars. A cross and I H S Monogram decorate the upper lunette.

This headstone is located within the old church ruins.

The Inscription Reads:

Here lieth the Body of patrick Doyle Dep[d] March 8th 1821 aged 77 Yers. lord have mercy on his soul Amen.

Surprisingly, the quality of the inscription far surpasses the quality of the ornamentation above it. This is a common feature of headstones portraying the Altar / Tabernacle theme. During the first half of the 19th century the quality of stone cutting at Kilnahue had diminished from the standard produced by the earlier masons, Cullen, Byrne, Donnelly, Kenney and Lee.

In all cases every effort has been made to reproduce the inscription as it appears on the headstone. The above Patrick was spelled with a small 'p'.

Kenna 1897, 1898 and 1903 Memorial Number 52

Height:	158 cm
Width:	72 cm
Depth:	10 cm

This elaborate white marble 'Revivalist Celtic' cross is located immediately north of the old church ruins. In common with similar type memorials, it dates from the late 19th / early 20th centuries.

Iconography:

The central motif portrays an image of Jesus displaying the Sacred Heart. Petal rosettes decorate the cross arms.

The manufacturer's name, M. Travers, Gorey, is located in the lower left corner.

The Inscription Reads:

Erected by Michael Kenna of Creagh in memory of his beloved daughter Mary Kate Kenna who died 20th Nov 1897 aged 18 years. Also his son William Kenna died 27th Feb 1898 aged 21 years. Also the above Michael Kenna died 26th March 1903 aged 64 years

The above inscription narrows the date of the headstone's erection to within a few years. It was obviously erected between the death of Mary Kate Kenna in late 1897 and the death of her father in early 1903. In the absence of precise erection dates, it is beneficial to the archaeologist or art historian to know the types of monument popular at any given time.

Fitzsimons 1869 and 1880 Memorial Number 53

Height:	160 cm
Width:	71 cm
Depth:	10 cm

Iconography:
A stylishly incised I H S motif is centrally located on the cross. No other ornamentation was noted.

The manufacturer's name, M. Travers, Gorey, is inscribed in the lower left corner.

The Inscription Reads:
Erected to the memory of Patrick Fitzsimons of Creagh who died 25th April 1880 aged 80 years Also his brother John Fitzsimons died 27th Dec 1869 Aged 67 years. This stone is erected by his son James Fitzsimons R.I.P.

This memorial is somewhat similar to Memorial Number 18, which records a burial in 1888. Both are by M. Travers, Gorey.

Toole 1816 Memorial Number 54

The headstone is 130 cm in height by 102 cm in width and is 8 cm in depth.

In common with many of these Altar / Tabernacle headstones, the inscription is still legible but the iconography is poorly preserved.

Iconography:

Iconography on the Toole headstone is similar to that portrayed on the Darcey 1809 Memorial Number 47. The crucified figure of Christ is centrally located within a domed portico, which is surmounted by the crossed I H S. A monstrance occurs on either side, flanked in turn by *ciboria*.

The Inscription Reads:

Erected by Tobias Toole in memory of his wife Mary Toole who depart[d] this life Jan[ry] 6th 1816 aged 43 years and also two of her children Rest in Peace.

Rocetor 1778 Memorial Number 55

Height: 62 cm
Width: 39 cm
Depth: 7 cm

This small headstone is damaged on the upper right hand corner.

Iconography:

A simple I H S motif surmounted by a large cross and set within a domed panel decorates the lunette on the Rocetor headstone.

The Inscription Reads:

Here lieth the Body of Dan^L Rocetor Dep^d March the 7th 1778 Ag^d 71 Y^rs Lord have mercy on his soul.

During the progress of the Kilnahue survey, the above headstone was first noted by Angela, whose maiden name was Rossiter, a likely spelling variation of Rocetor. Variances in the spelling of names, particularly prior to modern standardization, can confuse. MacLysaght[12] uses the surname Cullen, numerous at Kilnahue, as an example. During the 19th century variations in spelling included Quillen, Culhone, Colquhoun and Collen. He also refers to Irish American variations in spellings; in one case the headstones of six members of a McEneaney family provide six different spellings of the name.

---

[12] MacLysaght, E. 2007. *The Surnames of Ireland.* Irish Academic Press, Dublin. Pages x - xi

Cullon / Cullin 1796 Memorial Number 56

Measurements are 89 cm in height by 82 cm in width. Depth of the stone is 5 cm.

This headstone is signed by the mason, J. Byrne, beneath the iconography on the right.

Iconography:

The traditional portrayal of the crucifixion is featured on this example of Byrne's work. Christ is central to the scene; the serpent and death's head occur beneath His feet. Two figures flank the cross. Both are female and display halos. These represent Mary the mother of Jesus, facing outwards on the left and wearing a crown. Mary Magdalene occurs on the right in profile. The moon crescent and the sun flank the scene. Both are depicted with human faces as was customary. An I H S and arrowhead motif provide a border between the decoration and the inscription.

The Inscription Reads:

This stone was erected by John Cullon in memory of his wife Mary Cullin who dep^d this life Oct 21st 1796 Ag^d 50 yrs. Lord have mercy on her soul.

It is apparent that the same surname is spelled differently on the headstone.

Height is 88 cm, width is 93 cm, and depth is *circa* 5 cm.

This stone is signed by the mason, J. Byrne, beneath the moon crescent on the right.

Iconography:

The central figure of the crucified Christ occurs between two female figures. Mary, His mother, identified by her crown, stands on the left. She possibly holds a flower in her hands. Mary Magdalene is portrayed standing on the right. The serpent and death's head occur below Christ's feet, symbolizing His victory over evil and death. The moon crescent and sun in glory are neatly fitted at either side. An I H S and arrowhead motif decorate the border beneath.

The Inscription Reads:

Here lies the Body of Daniel Mc Daniel who Dep^d this life April 8th 1797 Ag^d 34 Y^{rs}. Also Anne Mc Daniel March 15th 1795 Ag^d 18 Y^{rs}

The McDaniel headstone iconography is practically identical to that on the Cullon Number 56 example, but it is in a far better state of preservation.

Dooley and Fitzgarield 1798 and 1801 Memorial Number 58

Height:	95 cm
Width:	72 cm
Depth:	5 cm

The decorated area on the Dooley headstone is in an extremely poor state of preservation.

Iconography:
Rubbings of the stone have identified it as belonging to the Altar / Tabernacle category. The central image, probably a cross, is located between porticos. It is not clear if there is an accompanying figure on the cross. A deeply incised crossed I H S motif is preserved above it. A monstrance, also incised by an I H S, occurs on either side.

The Inscription Reads:
Here lieth the body of Jam Dooley who dp this life Jan 5th 1798 Ag 23 yr. Also the Body of Maig Fitzgarield who departed Apr^l 20th 1801 Ag^d 15yr^s. Lord have mercy on their souls.

The spelling of the name Fitzgarield is reminiscent of the Gaelic version of the name.

It was not the mission of this survey to investigate the numbers of Irish speakers remaining in the area during the latter half of the 18th and pre-famine 19th centuries. However, even in areas of the country where Irish continued to be the dominant language during these periods, headstone inscriptions are generally in English. Irish language inscriptions are noted to occur in some areas during the latter years of the 19th century, due mainly to the renewed awareness of national identity.

O'Neill 1799 Memorial Number 59

Height: 93 cm
Width: 70 cm
Depth: 8 cm

Iconography:

The crucified figure of Christ is framed within a Neo-Classical style church or tabernacle. The columns, facade and roof are very similar in style to St Mary's Pro-Cathedral and to St Catherine's Church, Thomas Street, Dublin. An elaborate I H S is displayed above. Two smaller 'doorways' flank the central portico. A figure is portrayed in each, but without further detail it is impossible to identify them. Winged cherubs are displayed above both of these figures.

The O'Neill headstone is located within the church ruins and is signed by D. Cullen. He was either the son or nephew of the first Cullen but his work is not of the same quality.

The Inscription Reads:

Here Lieth the Body of Thomas O Neill who dep^d this life January the 28th 1799 aged 39 Years Also his Daughter Ann died July 16th 1799 aged 15 yrs. Lord have mercy on their souls Amen

The iconography is in the Neo-Classical style, which became popular on the continent towards the final quarter of the 18th century and quickly spread to Ireland and Britain.

The O'Neill headstone depiction of the crucified figure of Christ framed by a portico is by far the best preserved example of this iconography type at Kilnahue. These Altar / Tabernacle stones are not all the same. There are some major differences in design, but they all carry a common theme, are roughly contemporary and are generally very lightly cut.

Doyle 1766 Memorial Number 60

Height:	74 cm
Width:	54 cm
Depth:	6 cm

Iconography:

This is one of Cullen's simpler layouts. In the centre is the figure of the crucified Christ. A winged angel floats above the ground on either side. The hammer, which is usually found in association with other passion symbols, appears in isolation on the left.

A large I H S motif occurs below the cross.

This unsigned headstone is attributed to Cullen based on the style and the quality of the work.

The Inscription Reads:

Here Lieth the Body of Patrick Doyle Who Depart^{ed} this life the 17th day of November 1766 AG^D 47 years. Lord have mercy on his soul Amen.

There are several headstones at Kilnahue, and elsewhere, portraying the I H S motif, generally referred to as the Monogram. This is the most popular ornamentation used on Irish headstones since the mid 18th century and appears in various formats and styles. Had the above example been cut by anybody else, the depiction of the I H S motif would probably be counted among the ordinary and mundane. In Cullen's hands it becomes true vernacular Irish art.

Conor 1745 Memorial Number 61

Height is 77 cm, width 63 cm, and depth 18cm.

Iconography:

The granite Conor headstone displays a representation of the passion symbols together with the I H S motif surmounted by a cross. On the right the pincers holding a nail is noted and a dice is neatly fitted into the corner. The lance, ladder and hammer occur on the left, together with a bent nail. Two similar nails are placed above the uprights on the large letter 'H'.

The Inscription Reads in Capitals:

HERE LYETH Y^E BODY OF BRYAN CONOR WHO DEPARTED THIS LIFE IN THE YEAR 1745 AGED 74 YEARS. ALSO THE BODY OF MARY CONOR

Only two of the six granite headstones at Kilnahue are legible, the above Conor stone and Byrne Number 113. The letter 'N' is inverted on the Conor inscription but not on the Byrne memorial. Had the letter been inverted on both stones, it might have been suggested that both were by the same mason.

Kereuan 1765 Memorial Number 62

Height:	80 cm
Width:	58 cm
Depth:	10 cm

The inscription on this headstone is clear and easily read but the iconography is weak. The Kereuan memorial is one of three older limestone examples on the site.

Iconography:

The I H S Monogram surmounted by a cross is centrally located within a plain circle. Rubbings of the stone showed that no other decoration was applied.

The Inscription Reads:

Here lies the Body of Bridget Kereuan who Departed this life April the 8th 1765 Aged 27 yea^{rs}

Spellings of personal names are as on the headstones. It is interesting to note how the stone cutter lifted the final letters of 'years' to fit the line. This practice was quiet common on headstones. There are also many examples at Kilnahue and elsewhere of word clipping. Departed is commonly written as 'dep^d' and years as 'y^{rs}'. Stonecutters usually charged by the number of letters, but apart from cost, the practice also served to fit long inscriptions into a confined space.

Kelley 1727, 1745 and 1762 Memorial Number 63

Height: 94 cm
Width: 63 cm
Depth: 8 cm

The decorated area extends approximately 20 cm from the top.

Iconography:

Iconography employed on the Kelley headstone consists of the traditional I H S motif surmounted by a cross and the crucified Christ. A ladder and lance are evident on the left as well as a pincers holding a nail. A hammer and nail are depicted on the right. All of these implements are associated with the crucifixion and referred to as passion symbols.

There is no evidence of a mason's name.

The Inscription Reads:

Here Lieth the Body of Cornelis Kelley who Departed this Life in the year 1727 AG^d 51 year. All so John Kelley Departed ye 5th of April 1745 AG^d 20. Peter Kelley departed Decenber 17th 1762 AG^d 37 years

The inscription on the Kelley headstone records three burials between 1727 and 1762. It is often worth looking at the style of lettering in order to estimate when the stone was erected. In many instances, date of death and date of headstone erection may be decades apart. In the above case, based on the uniformity of the lettering and 1760s style of decoration, it is probable that the headstone was erected following the final burial.

This headstone has certain similarities to the later Stanton Memorial Number 72 and to Byrne Number 100 and may have influenced their design. .

The Woodbyrne headstone measures 92 cm in height by 82 cm in width and is approximately 6 cm in depth. Slight damage has occurred on the upper moulding.

This headstone is signed by the mason, J. Byrne, in the decorated area on the right. The stone is located within the church ruins.

Iconography:

There is a slight variation between this stone and other examples of Byrne's work at Kilnahue. The figure of the crucified Christ is centrally located with Mary, His mother, identified by her crown, and the sun in glory on the left. Mary Magdalene and the moon crescent are set to the right. The lower section of the cross shaft is flanked by decorative pillars. Possible sycomore figs, doum palms or olive trees occur in the otherwise vacant corner spaces, giving an eastern flavour to the scene. The I H S and arrowhead motif border separates the decorative area from the inscription.

The Inscription Reads:

Here lies the Body of Mary Woodbyrne who Dep[d] this life March 16th 1792 Ag[d] 18 Y[rs] Lord have Mercy on her Soul

Illegible Memorial Number 65

This small granite headstone measures 56 cm in height by 60 cm in width by 21 cm in depth. The decorated area extends 25 cm from the top. Iconography consists of the I H S Monogram flanked on either side by a disk-like feature. The inscription is illegible.

The iconography is similar to that on the Hayden Number 41 headstone and might therefore be the work of the same mason and be of a similar date. Dating the stone to the mid 18th century is also supported by comparison with the other granite stones on site.

It is difficult to determine the contemporary cost of headstones in Ireland without appropriate records. Burgess[13], in his *English Churchyard Memorials*, cites some English examples but it is likely that Irish rural prices were much lower. He records locally cut stone as costing about three shillings a foot and letter cutting a penny each during the eighteenth century. An Irish labourer's pay was between four to six pence a day at the time. A small two foot high professionally cut headstone and short inscription would cost more that a month's income and was therefore probably beyond reach for many people.

---

[13] *Ibid.*, pages 271 - 278

Byrne 1773 Memorial Number 66

The Byrne headstone stands 110 cm in height by 82 cm in width and is 9 cm in depth.

Iconography:

A large I H S motif surmounted by a cross almost fills the lunette. A trowel, possibly a symbol of the deceased's trade, occurs to the left of the cross.

The Inscription Reads:

Here lieth the Body of John Byrne who departed this life Octob[r] y[e] 6 th 1773 Aged 63 years Also the Body of Mary Byrne his first wife Aged 36 years. Requiescant in Pace

Cut by John Byrne Grand Son is inscribed immediately beneath the decoration. Based on the occurrence of a trade symbol in the lunette and the signing of the stone, it is probable that both the deceased John Byrne and his grandson John were masons. Longfield[14] suggests that the family of the stone cutter James Byrne (see Memorial Numbers 27, 35, 37, 56, 57, 64, 73, 87 and 123) were also involved in the headstone business but there is no direct evidence to confirm that John or his grandfather were of the same family.

It is a rare occurrence to find a symbol of the deceased's trade on a headstone in the region. The practice of including occupation symbols was more usually observed in Britain and in the northern counties.

---

[14] Longfield, A. 1945. Some 18th Century Irish Tombstones (continued). III. James Byrne and his School. *Journal of the Royal Society of Antiquarians of Ireland* 75, 76 – 84.

This Byrne headstone stands 93 cm in height by 55 cm in width and is 10 cm in depth.

Iconography:

A simple I H S motif surmounted by a cross occurs within a rayed circle.

The Inscription Reads:

Here lyeth ye Body of John Byrne who departed this life the 17th day of March 1744 aged 83 years

Based on John Byrne's age and date of death, he was the earliest recorded birth at Kilnahue, being born in 1661.

This headstone is in close proximity to that of John Byrne who died in 1773 and was inscribed by his grandson. It is therefore possible that both stones belong to the same family. It is not known if they were related to the later James Byrne whose work is signed at Kilnahue later in the century.

Uninscribed Memorial Number 68

Height: 57 cm
Width: 28 cm
Depth: 6 cm

This is an example of an uninscribed homemade or vernacular headstone or grave marker. It occurs immediately left of a similarly cut but inscribed stone dated 1757. It is probable that both stones are roughly contemporary.

The headstone is reminiscent of an Early Medieval Irish cross-slab in style and outline but of inferior workmanship. Kilnahue is an ancient site and perhaps a cross-slab once existed in the vicinity and that the carver was aware of it, or perhaps, he had travelled and seen examples elsewhere.

Iconography:

The stone displays two crosses. One occurs in the upper division within a circle, which is set within a panel. The upper part of the panel is decorated by a simply incised scroll. A second basic cross is incised beneath, decorating the lower area.

Early Medieval cross-slab at *Cill Rialaigh*, Co. Kerry.

Photograph: Gerry Mullins.

Wadic 1757 Memorial Number 69

Height:	50 cm
Width:	44 cm
Depth:	7 cm

This is another homemade or vernacular headstone. The iconography and inscription are roughly cut but legible.

Iconography:

A large Greek cross, surmounting a small 'H', is set between the letters I and S.

The Inscription Reads in Capitals:

HERE LYETH YE BODY OF MARY WADIC DECEASED IV NOV IN THE YEAR 1757 IN AGE 42 YEAR.

This is the only headstone at Kilnahue to use Roman Numerals. Note that the 4 of the date is written as IV.

All the early headstones at Kilnahue employed capital letters in the inscription. Burgess[15] states that this practice was changing in England during the early years of the 18th century when capitals were abandoned in favour of what he terms 'roundhead'. He also suggests that the new style was spread by commerce and trade and was related to the growing popularity of calligraphy.

---

[15] Burgess, F. 1963. *English Churchyard Memorials*. Lutterworth Press, London. Pages 206 – 216.

No Name Memorial Number 70

This unusually shaped and partially buried headstone extends 41 cm above the ground. It measures 52 cm in width and is 5 cm in depth.

Iconography:

An I H S motif surmounted by a cross serves as the central decoration. This is flanked on the right by a pincers holding a nail and on the left by a ladder. The secondary iconography is symbolic of the passion of Jesus.

The Inscription Reads:

Here Lyeth the Body of

Because the stone is deeply buried, only the upper section of the inscription is legible. However, judging from its appearance, it seems as if nothing more was inscribed. Perhaps the inscription was unfinished.

Angel Memorial Number 71

This small statue of an angel stands in the churchyard. There is no associated inscription or date. But it is considered a fitting memorial to the countless numbers throughout the centuries whose burials are unrecorded on a conventional headstone.

This headstone stands 83 cm in height by 58 cm in width and is 3 – 5 cm in depth.

Iconography:

The principal motif comprises a splayed cross surmounting the I H S Monogram within a rayed circle. A pincers holding a nail occurs on the right as if floating in mid-air. A ladder and lance occur on the left. The lunette is further decorated by a checkerboard pattern.

The Inscription reads:

Here Lieth the Body of Bryan Stanton Who Dep^d this Life January the 6th 1773 AG^d 60 years. Also Anestas Stanton Died April the 20th 1778 AG^d 65 years. Lord have mercy on their Souls Amen.

There is no mason's name on the Stanton headstone, but it remains one of the most attractive memorials at Kilnahue. The style is somewhat similar to the Kelley Memorial Number 63 and to Byrne Number 100.

Murphy 1804 and 1807 Memorial Number 73

Height:	122 cm
Width:	79 cm
Depth:	6 - 7 cm

Iconography:

The crucified Christ occurs as the central motif. The serpent and death's head are illustrated beneath the cross. Mary is portrayed on the left, identified by her crown as Queen of Heaven; beside her is the sun in glory. Mary Magdalene is portrayed on the right with the moon crescent. Both the sun and moon are represented with human faces, as was customary. The I H S Monogram and diamond motifs decorate the border area between the iconography and inscription.

This stone is signed by the mason J. Byrne beneath the iconography on the left.

The Inscription Reads:

Here lies the Body of Elizabeth Murphy who Dep^d this life Jan 16th 1807 Ag^d 66 Y^{rs} Also her Daughter Elenor Murphy Augt 13th 1804 Ag^d 21 Y^{rs} Lord Have Mercy on their Souls.

This headstone is typical of Byrne's work. At Kilnahue he produced three basic patterns. Monument Numbers 35, 56 and 57 and the above Murphy headstone portray Mary facing, rather than in profile, resulting in a more attractive perspective. On Monuments Number 27, 64 and 87 he portrayed both figures in profile and uniformed figures are included on Monument Numbers 37 and 123. Byrne was obviously popular, for the numbers of headstones produced by his business, which probably included family and apprentices, far surpass production throughout the south eastern region by any other mason[16].

---

[16] Longfield, A. 1945. Some 18th Century Irish Tombstones (continued). III. James Byrne and his school. Journal of the Royal Society of Antiquaries of Ireland 75, 76 - 84.

Brislawn 1778 Memorial Number 74

Height:	146 cm
Width:	72 cm
Depth:	4 cm

Iconography:

Cullen has departed from his customary crucifixion scene on this 1778 Brislawn headstone.

Although he includes the traditional figure of Christ on the cross as a central motif, in this instance it is flanked by winged cherubs. The cross is placed on a plinth or pedestal. The I H S Monogram appears below.

This headstone is signed beneath the iconography on the right by the mason, D. Cullen.

The Inscription Reads:

Here Lieth the Body of Farrell Brislawn Dep^d Dec the 25th 1778 Ag^d 63 yr^s also his son Miles Dep^d Oct the 13th 1778 Ag^d 21 yr^s Lord have mercy on their Souls Amen

Sometimes when reading headstone inscriptions we forget the human element to the stories. This stone records the death of a father and son within weeks of each other. It is noted that inscriptions during this period are very straightforward and state facts devoid of any personal comment. These came much later, about the mid 19th century, when the terms 'deeply regretted' and 'in loving memory' became accepted. Based on headstone inscriptions it often seems that death was more acceptable and viewed as a part of normal life prior to the mid 19th century.

Brislane 1766 Memorial Number 75

Height: 81 cm
Width: 60 cm
Depth: 9 cm

Iconography:
The traditional figure of Christ on the cross occurs as the central motif. Mary, His mother, is portrayed in profile on the right, crowned and holding a rosary beads. Two winged angels occur behind her. On the left a winged angel floats above the ground. A human figure stands behind a table on which there is a chalice, possibly representing the mass and sacrifice. A small damaged figure occurs in the corner, possibly holding a thurible. The sun in glory decorates the left finial; damage has occurred to that on the right. An I H S motif is cut beneath the cross.

This unsigned stone is attributed to Cullen based on style and quality.

The Inscription Reads:
Here Lyeth the Body of Owen Brishlane Who Departed this Life ye 14th of Feburary 1766 agd 76 years

The headstones of Owen Brishlane and Farrell Brislawn stand side by side in the churchyard. It is presumed that both were members of the same family. However, it allows an insight into the variations found in 18th century spelling, even when both headstones are assigned to the same mason.

Although the stone is unsigned, this is by far the most sophisticated of Cullen's headstones at Kilnahue. Unfortunately the figures on the left are somewhat weathered and damaged.

Masterson 1727 Memorial Number 76

Height: 74 cm
Width: 33 cm
Depth: 8 cm

This is another typical example of a vernacular headstone. It seems that the Masterson memorial was decorated and inscribed whilst in its present condition, as the wording is not damaged and follows the uneven line of the stone.

Iconography:
Decoration comprises a simple I H S motif surmounted by a cross.

The Inscription in Capitals Reads:
HERE LIETH THE BODY OF JOHN MASTERSON WHO DEPARTEDT THIS LIFE ANNO DOMINIE 1727

Although the Heydon headstone Number 41 displays an earlier date, 1716, it is likely that this Masterson memorial is the oldest inscribed example at Kilnahue. The stone seems to be a transitional type, occurring between the rough markers and the later professionally produced memorials. Examples like this are useful when tracing the development of the headstone. It is also the only inscription on the site using the Latin term *Anno Domini*, meaning 'in the year of our Lord', which in common with the word 'departed', is incorrectly spelled.

Masterson 1738 Memorial Number 77

Height:	79 cm
Width:	48 cm
Depth:	2 cm

This headstone again is of the homemade or vernacular variety.

Iconography:

Iconography consists of a large H beneath a cross, which in turn occurs above a smaller version of a similar motif. This smaller motif depicts a T shaped cross.

The origins and meaning of the I H S Monogram were not seemingly understood by the mason who carved the stone. This is strange, especially as the earlier Masterson Number 76 beside it carried a proper representation of the I H S motif.

A domed panel was incised on the face of the stone but seems to serve no purpose apart from decoration as it does not confine the inscription.

The Inscription Reads in Capitals:

HEERE LIEST THE BODY OF JAMES MASTERSON WHO DISHCID IN THE YEAR 1738

Based on date and style, this is likely to have been the second inscribed headstone at Kilnahue, making the Masterson family the first to introduce the idea. There is no evidence to suggest that headstones were officially removed from rural Irish medieval parish churchyards in order to make room for replacements. It is therefore probable that those currently occurring on these sites are original and were the first inscribed examples to be erected.

Fragmented Memorial Number 78

This damaged memorial is located within the old church ruins.

The preserved portion of the stone measures 87 cm in height, 90 cm in width and is 7 cm in depth. There is no surviving decoration or inscription, apart from *Req^t in Pace Amen* inscribed along the base, and the missing upper portion was not found lying in the churchyard.

Field archaeology requires the investigation of negative as well as positive features. The purpose of archaeology is to preserve by record. It may be of interest to a future generation to know exactly the state and condition of the headstones at Kilnahue during 2010 - 2011. There are currently only two headstones in the above condition, Memorial Numbers 23 and the above Number 78. The need to create a record is also the reason that stone measurements were recorded. Pre-famine headstones were not uniformly produced. Perhaps at a future date when all the iconography and inscriptions have deteriorated beyond recognition, some stones at least might by identified by their dimensions.

This broken headstone measures 100 cm in height by 91 cm in width and is 7cm in depth.

Iconography:

The I H S motif surmounted by a cross occurs within a rayed circle, which in turn is encircled by a *gloria* scroll. *Ciboria* within domed panels flank the central decoration.

The Inscription Reads:

Erec^d by Patrick Cullen Toreduff in memr of his wife Catherine Cullen who dep^d this life decr the 16th 1839 agd 37 years also his daughter Mary dep^d april 1st 1840 aged 11 months Also his daughter Elizabeth april 20 1810 aged 15 yrs

The above inscription is a rare pre-famine example of naming a deceased child. The chronological sequences of burials might suggest a second marriage. But it is not unknown for a mason to cut an incorrect date.

Wadic 1743, 1757, 1767 and 1780 Memorial Number 80

The Wadic ledger is lying, probably disturbed, in a central location within the church ruins. There was no iconography identified on the stone. It also proved difficult to read the inscription, which was eventually only partially deciphered.

The stone ledger measures 181 cm by 81 cm by 18cm in depth.

The Partially Deciphered Inscription Reads:
Here lieth the body of Cornelius Wadic ....1743. Here lieth the body ....1757 Aged 82 ....Felix Wadic ..... March 3rd 1767......Also his son Michael Wadic who departed this life the 31st day of December 1780 aged 64.

This memorial type is generally referred to as a ledger. Rather than an upstanding headstone a flat recumbent slab was used. They can be notoriously difficult to read, as unlike the headstone, the ledger is constantly exposed to the elements. Large ledgers were naturally more expensive than the ordinary headstone. Prices were based on size and on the number of letters inscribed. Ledgers no doubt had a status value.

Memorial Number 81

This small stone is located within the old church ruin.

The stone stands 52 cm in height by 30 cm in width and is only about 3 cm in depth. There is no inscription or decoration apart from a T shaped cross, which extends 17 cm from the top.

Bolger and Kavanah 1804, 1806, 1817 and 1819
Memorial Number 82

This table tomb stands on four plinths and measures 183 cm in length by 90 cm in width and is 11 cm in depth.

Iconography:

A large crossed I H S Monogram covers the upper section of the slab.

The Inscription Reads:

Here lies the body of John Bolger who departed this life the 9th of June 1804 Aged 25 yrs Lord have mercy on his soul Amen Also the body of Mick Kavanah depd August 21st 1806 aged 19 years Also the body Dainyal Bolger departed November 19th 1817 Aged 55 Also his father John Bolger Departed May 1st 1819 age 99.

In common with ledger type memorials, it is often difficult to read a table tomb, as the inscription has had greater exposure to the elements than ordinary headstones.

John Bolger, aged 99, was the oldest deceased person recorded at Kilnahue.

Bolger and Dempsey 1801 and 1828 Memorial Number 83

Height:	141 cm
Width:	84 cm
Depth:	6 cm

This finely cut sandstone is in excellent condition, attractively laid out and well proportioned.

Iconography:
Decorative motifs consist of the traditional I H S motif surmounted by a cross within a rayed circle.

The Inscription Reads:
Here lies the Body of Catherine Bolger alias Dempsey who Dep^d this life the 1ST of April 1801 aged 35 Y^{rs} Lord have mercy on her Soul Amen Also her husban^d Con Bolger Dep^d this life March 23rd 1828 aged 75 yrs. Requiescant in Pace Amen. The words *Also her two children* are inscribed at the base of the stone.

In comparison with the superbly sculpted stones of the well-known masons, many of the other examples currently look plain and mundane. Although much of Burgess' 1963 book, *English Churchyard Memorials*, is not relevant to rural Ireland, perhaps his statement regarding the painting of headstones has some significance[17].

In this book several sources are referenced concerning the painting of lettering, which is still a common practice, and evidence is given that in some English localities headstones were whitewashed regularly and decorative motifs were painted accordingly. In Ireland, there is evidence that medieval stone sculpture was commonly painted, including the ancient Irish high crosses [18]. There is no reason to suggest that Irish headstones were not also painted when newly erected.

---

17. Page 275
18. Henry, Francoise, 1964. *Irish High Crosses*. The Cultural Relations Committee, Dublin.

Bulger 1794 Memorial Number 84

Height:	105 cm
Width:	87 cm
Depth:	6 cm

Some moulding has been damaged on the upper section of the stone.

Iconography:

Christ is portrayed on the cross below the I N R I. The serpent and death's head occur at His feet. Mary, Christ's mother, is on the left, identified by her crown. Behind her occur the sun in glory and a probable olive or palm tree. Mary Magdalene is represented by the figure on the right with the moon crescent and an olive or palm tree. An I H S and arrowhead motif decorates the border.

This headstone is signed by the mason, M. Kenney, beneath the decoration on the right.

The Inscription Reads:

Here lies the Body of James Bulger who dep^d this life Oct 7th 1794 ag^{e}d 84 Yrs. Lord have mercy on his Soul.

The words '*also the body*' are inscribed near the base but no other inscription was apparent.

Stones by Martin Kenney and James Byrne are very similar. They are also roughly contemporary. It is not known if Kenney was originally an apprentice of Byrne or vice versa.

MB Memorial Number 85

This small sandstone slab measured 57 cm in height by 36 cm in width and 8 cm in depth. At present it leans slightly forward and to the right.There is no inscription apart from the letter M and an inverted B beneath the incised cross.

Memorial Number 85 might seem a pretentious title to put upon such an insignificant little stone. Looking at it from a 21st century perspective it is difficult to understand its relevance and significance to the person who erected it, or to the society to which that person belonged. In common with Number 15, the undated Cauanach memorial, it seems to be one step removed from a rough stone grave marker. Harold Mythum, an archaeological theorist at the University of York,[19] suggested that some early stones were simply used as family grave markers on which there was never any intention of recording further inscriptions. Contemporary culture did not consider it important that every burial should be inscribed. Everybody in the parish probably knew M.B., knew where the plot was located, and knew who was buried there. The same may be said regarding uninscribed rough stone markers. Ireland had long been an oral rather than a literate society.

---

[19] Mythum, H. 2003 - 04. Artefact biography as an approach to material culture: Irish gravestones as a material form of genealogy. *The Journal of Irish Archaeology* Volumes X11 and XIII. Wordwell, Bray.

Breen 1787 Memorial Number 86

The headstone of Patrick Breen stands 98 cm in height by 80 cm in width. It is approximately 4 cm in depth.

Iconography:

This unsigned stone depicts the figure of Christ on the cross and the serpent at the his feet, flanked by the usual two figures. But only the figure on the left has a halo. It is presumed that the carver intended to depict Mary the mother of Jesus and Mary Magdalene, as was customary. Although the figure on the cross is reasonably well-rendered, the two other figures are not realistic: they are disproportionate and their faces are amateurish. The moon crescent and sun in glory also appear in the scene.

The border separating iconography and inscription is quiet decorative, combining a central I H S, arrowhead and checkerboard motifs.

The Inscription Reads:

Here lies the Body of patric^k Breen Who dep^d this life fe^{bry} the 16th 1787 Ag'd 78 Y^{rs} . Lord have mercy on his sou^l

It was noted that the letter S is inverted in both occurrences in the inscription.

This headstone stands 126 cm in height by 82 cm in width and varies between 3 and 7 cm in depth.

It is signed by the mason, J. Byrne, beneath the decoration on the left.

Iconography:

This is one of Byrne's typical headstones. The crucified Christ is portrayed as the central figure. Mary, His mother, and Mary Magdalene occur on either side. Both display halos around their heads. Decorative pillars flank the cross shaft. The moon crescent and sun in glory, both represented with the customary face, are depicted on opposite sides. Small palm trees fill the corner spaces. An I H S and arrowhead motifs decorate the border area below the iconography.

The Inscription Reads:

Here lies the Body of Catharine Breen who Dep^d this life April 3^d 1799 Ag^d 23 Y^{rs} Lord have Mercy on her Soul

Decorative pillars flank the lower section of the cross shaft on both Memorials Number 64, also by Byrne, and the above Number 87.

Kain 1778, 1810 and 1830 Memorial Number 88

Height:	120 cm
Width:	76 cm
Depth:	6 cm

Iconography:

The Kain memorial conforms roughly to the Altar / Tabernacle type.

A monstrance, altar and candelabra are framed within a portico beneath a dome. These in turn are enclosed by a second portico beneath a similar dome, which is decorated by a large *gloria* scroll. A monstrance occurs on either side of the second portico, set within domed panels.

This is a particularly complex assortment of decorative detail.

The Inscription Reads:

Erec^td by Barnaby Kain in Memory of his Father Edward Kain Dep^d this life March 15th 1778 Aged 33 Yrs. Also 3 of Barnby Kain Children Edward Depar^d Augu^st 11th 1810 Aged 6 Yrs. Also his mother Catheine Kain 21st apr^l 1830 aged 78 Y^rs And also 5 of his children. Barnaby Kain Dp^d (blank space) *18* (blank space) *Aged* (blank space) *Yrs. Requieseant in Pace*

The inscription may be slightly confusing but it is evident that the erector of the stone, Barnaby Kain, had the inscription for his own departure date partially prepared at the time of the headstone's manufacture. These blank spaces were never filled.

Nouland and Crean 1799, 1804 and 1816 Memorial Number 89

Height:	123 cm
Width:	99 cm
Depth:	8 cm

The decorative detail in the lunette is weak. Only the central crucified figure is still plainly visible.

Iconography:

This headstone again conforms to the Altar / Tabernacle type. Jesus on the cross is centrally depicted and flanked by two figures. These are likely to represent Mary and Mary Magdalene. The scene is set within a Neo-Classical portico beneath a large I H S motif. A monstrance and *ciborium* are set at each side of the central iconography.

The Inscription Reads:

This stone erecte^d by France Nouland in memory of her Father Mich^l Crean who Dp^d this life Augst 13th 1799 Aged 61 yr^s Also the Body of Mich^l Crean his Son Dep^d Decr 21st 1804 Ag^d 27 Y^{rs}. Also the body of Frances Nouland who Dep^d this life April 1816 Agd 51 yrs. Lord have Mercy on their Souls.

Although this example is not signed, two of the Altar / Tabernacle stones at Kilnahue are signed by the makers. Memorial Number 59, O'Neill 1799, is signed by the second D. Cullen and Memorial Number 95, Hanlon 1816, is signed by Jas Walsh, Carlow. There are 16 headstones at Kilnahue portraying various Altar / Tabernacle scenes, 15 of these are likely to have been erected between 1800 and 1830. Unfortunately the poor preservation of iconography on these Altar / Tabernacle stones does not allow for detailed comparisons of either decoration or of style. The sixteenth stone, Number 121, records five burials beginning in 1864 and is therefore not likely to have been done by the same stone cutters.

Uninscribed Memorial Number 90

This small sandstone stands immediately behind the Crean Number 89 headstone. It measures 84 cm in height by 47 cm in width and is 5 cm in depth.

To comment on the original function of this stone is pure conjecture. There is a slight gap between it and the Crean headstone. As it was policy during this survey that no interference should occur with anything on the site, only a casual inspection of the eastern face was undertaken. There was no apparent inscription.

It is understood that for convenience, initial inscriptions were most likely to have been cut by the masons on their premises. Subsequent inscriptions were inscribed in the churchyard. Headstone Number 90 is relatively small and comparatively easily transported. It is conceivable that it was transported to the churchyard and never finished.

It is also possible that some masons provided a temporary or movable headstone to be used as a marker.

Toole and Corrigan 1776 and 1794 Memorial Number 91

Height:	111 cm
Width:	87 cm
Depth:	9cm

Iconography

The crucified figure of Christ occurs as the central motif. The serpent and death's head are set beneath His feet. Mary and Mary Magdalene flank the cross in profile; both are depicted with halos. The sun in glory is set on the left and the moon crescent on the right, both with a human face as was traditional. A small palm tree occurs in each lower corner. A large I H S and arrowhead motif decorates the border between the iconography and inscription.

This headstone is signed by the mason, M. Kenney, directly beneath the figure on the right.

The Inscription Reads:

Here lies the body of Hugh Toole who dep^d this life July 13th 1776 agd 43 yrs. Also Honorha Toole alias Corrigan July 15th 1794 agd 59 yrs. Lord have mercy on their souls.

Two of Kenney's headstones, Number 1 and the above Number 91, record burials in 1767 and in 1776 respectively. Byrne's earliest recorded burial inscription at Kilnahue was in 1768, (Monument Number 35). It is probable that all of these burials were recorded retrospectively, and that the headstones are contemporary with later burials.

Uninscribed Memorial Number 92

This rough uninscribed stone is set close to the western churchyard boundary. Measurements are 69 cm in height by 50 cm in width by 7 – 9 cm in depth.

Reference was made when commenting on the number of rough stones at Kilnahue, (see Memorial Number 2), to the tradition of using stones from the church ruins as burial markers. The above stone displays a probable bolt socket, indicating that it was used elsewhere, but of course not necessarily in the old church. It is located close to the old churchyard entrance and was possibly used in the gateway. But it was certainly moved and reset, as the current location of the proposed socket is of little use whether vertical or horizontal.

The occurrence of the proposed socket is only of passing interest, but it illustrates the advantages of recording everything.

Uninscribed Iron Memorial Number 93

Measurements are 106 cm in height by 58 cm wide at the arms. These are roughly similar dimensions to those of Iron Cross Monument Number 40. The style is also very similar, which suggests that both crosses were forged by the same person. Unfortunately, in common with Memorials Number 44 and the smaller iron cross Number 111, there was no identification mark or inscription identified.

The cross is set in a concrete plinth, which is now partially buried.

Murphy 1894, 1898 and 1933 Memorial Number 94

The headstone measures 97 cm in height by 66 cm in width and is 10 cm in depth.

This headstone is signed at the base by the manufacturer, Doyle, Bunclody.

Iconography:
An elaborate interlace I H S motif set within a circle forms the central ornamentation on the headstone.

The Inscription Reads in Capitals:
ERECTED BY DENIS MURPHY GOREY IN MEMORY OF HIS FATHER JAMES MURPHY DIED DEC 4TH 1894 AGED 65 YRS. HIS MOTHER CATHERINE MURPHY DIED AUG 29TH 1898 AGED 62 YRS. AND HIS BROTHER JOHN MURPHY DIED FEB 6TH 1933 AGE 71 YRS.

The I H S motif is similar to those depicted on Monuments Numbers 9 and 32.

Height: 120 cm
Width: 90 cm
Depth: 10 cm

Iconography:
The central motif portrays a monstrance set upon an altar. A crossed I H S above a heart is incised on its face. Candelabra stand at either side. The altar and furnishings occur within a Classical portico, which is decorated overhead by a monstrance, again displaying an I H S motif. This is flanked by two angels playing musical instruments. *Ciboria* occur at either side of the main design.

The aforementioned ornamentation occurs within a very stylized rayed penannular circle. A *gloria* scroll is spread beneath. Smaller *ciboria* fill the corners beneath the headstone shoulders.

The stone is signed beneath the decorated area by the marker, Jas Walsh, Barrack Street, Carlow.

The Inscription Reads:
Erected by David Hanlon of Castletown in memory of his wife Bridget Hanlon who Dep^d this life January the 20th 1816 aged 44 years Also his daughter Mary Hanlon who dep^d this life May the 16th 1816 aged 22 years

Inscribed at the Back of Stone:
Be patient friends, wipe away your tears, here we must lie until Christ appears. When he comes we expect to rise to a life that never dies.

Kerin 1752 Memorial Number 96

Height:	64 cm
Width:	49 cm
Depth:	5 cm

Unfortunately there is some damage to the upper right corner of this headstone.

Iconography:

A slight plinth occurs on the H bar to support the cross. This became a standard feature of headstone ornamentation. There may have been an abandoned attempt to form a cross from the letter 'I' and the letter 'S' is noticeably falling forward.

The Inscription Reads in Capitals:

HERE LYETH THE BODY OF DENNIS KERIN WHO DEPARTED THIS LIFE IN THE YEAR 1752 AGE 50

The 'S' of Dennis is regularly cut; the 'S' of 'this' is tilting forward.

The above inscription records the burial of a single male. Similar recordings seem to be reasonably plentiful during the mid 18th century, and indeed during later periods. The information inscribed on these headstones might present a research opportunity into the associations between memorial type, decoration and demographic groups. This could be done by parish, barony, county, or by any easily definable region. The scope of such a survey is practically limitless. Demographic groups could be isolated according to any desired criteria. Monument type and decoration could be defined by principal and secondary artwork e.g. the I H S accompanied by a rayed circle, *gloria* scroll or passion symbols. Age at death is also important, especially in the pre 1841 era, prior to the first census. As with Grogan's survey (see Memorial Number 36), further research might show surprising and interesting results.

Nicholoson 1844, 1845, 1868, 1877 and 1882
Memorial Number 97

Height: 157 cm
Width: 95 cm
Depth: 10 cm

Iconography:
The iconography on this stone is very simple. A stylized bracelet cross within a decorative panel occurs between two small crossed I H S motifs.

Both the Nicholoson and Travers Number 120 headstones are very similar in style and, together with the Byrne Memorial Number 117, are the only examples at Kilnahue to exhibit Gothic architectural influences.

The Inscription Reads:
Erected by George Nicholoson of Gorey in memory of his beloved father Samuel Nicholoson who dep^d this life 10th Dec 1845 aged 58 years. Also his beloved mother Mary Nicholoson who departed this life 13th Feb 1868 aged 61 years. Also his brother Michael Nicholoson who departed this life 1st Feb 1844 aged 15 years. Also the Boye George Nicholoson died 24th March 1877 aged 51 yrs. His sister Eliza died 12th July 1882 aged 60 years.

The back of this headstone is inscribed with a verse from the Old Testament's Second Book of Maccabees Chapter 12, Verse 46: *It is a holy and wholesome thought to pray for the dead that they may be loosed from their sins. 2. Mac. XII. 46.*

The same biblical passage occurs on the back of Monument Number 120.

Cain 1772 Memorial Number 98

Height:	93 cm
Width:	68 cm
Depth:	7 cm

Iconography:

A simple I H S motif surmounted by a cross occurs within a rayed half circle and is separated from the inscription by an arrowhead motif.

The same type of border arrowhead motif was later used by the mason James Byrne on his passion symbol headstones.

The Inscription Reads:

Here lieth the Body of James cain Who dep^d this life Apr the 3rd 1772 ag^d 60 yrs. Lord Have mercy on his soul

Some headstones provide a lot of information to a genealogist in search of a family tree, a good example being the information available from the Nolan / Byrne Memorial Number 12. But the James Cain headstone provides practically nothing. There is no record of the person who had the stone erected, no place of residence is mentioned, and there is no record of subsequent burials. However, a tomb in County Monaghan that recorded one burial in 1677 was found upon opening to contain about 20 bodies[20], proving that one recorded name does not necessarily mean one burial.

---

[20]McCormick, F. 1983. The symbols of death and the tomb on John Forster in Tydavnet, Co. Monaghan. *Clogher Record* 11, 273 – 286.

Uninscribed Memorial Number 99

Height:	54 cm
Width:	20 cm
Depth:	8 cm

This uninscribed rough stone is included as an example of the several that occur at Kilnahue.

The decision to include a sample of the rough uninscribed stones at Kilnahue is consistent with current archaeological practice. Archaeology has its roots in 17th and 18th century antiquarianism. This was largely concerned with providing artefacts for collectors and museum display. Little notice was taken of the ordinary and mundane. However, the evolution of archaeological thought has tended to place more emphasis on knowledge and on the understanding of the social process. Interpreting the mundane as well as the spectacular can be beneficial to the collection of knowledge[21]. Prior to the 1960s, according to Tarlow[22], many archaeologists failed to note 'divisions within social groups' and Johnson[23] stated that archaeologists were so busy sorting artefacts that they 'often seemed to ignore human beings'. To ignore the rough stones at Kilnahue, including the above Memorial Number 99, would be to ignore the people who erected it and also to ignore those who are buried beneath it.

---

[21]Binford, L. 1972. *An Archaeological Perspective*. Seminar Press, New York. Page 128.

[22]Tarlow, S. 1999. *Bereavement and Commemoration: an archaeology of mortality*. Blackwell, Oxford. Page 10.

[23] Johnson, M. 1999. *Archaeology Theory*. Blackwell, Oxford. Page 21.

Byrne 1775, 1791 and 1797 Memorial Number 100

Height:	147 cm
Width:	77 cm
Depth:	6 cm

Iconography:

An incised I H S motif surmounted by a cross occurs within a rayed circle. Some symbols of the passion including the ladder, pincers holding a nail, hammer and lance occur on the right. A winged cherub is depicted on the left.

The headstone is located within the old church ruin.

The Inscription Reads:

Here lieth the Body of Miles Byrne Who Departed this life April the 5th 1775 AG d 87 years. The Lord have mercy on his soul. And Mary Byrne his Grandchild and her sister Cathorine Depd this life Jan r 20th 1791 aged 17 yrs also his Son Patrick Byrne depd this life Febr 18th 1797 aged 70 Yrs.

Based on the above inscription, Miles Byrne was born in 1688, the same year in which the Catholic King James II was deposed from the throne in favour of William III. Miles Byrne's early years witnessed the resulting Williamite Wars in Ireland, including the Battle of the Boyne, the Siege of Limerick and the Battle of Aughrim.

The preserved portion of this headstone stands at 127 cm in height, 89 cm in width, and is 6 cm in depth.

The stone is signed by the mason, Patk Donnelly.

Iconography:

Although the upper section of the headstone is missing, the iconography employed is obvious. The base of the cross and the serpent flanked by two figures is intact. The sun in glory is preserved on the left. An I H S occurs beneath.

The Inscription Reads:

This Stone is erected by John Finnell for the use of his fameley. Here lies the Body of Margerey fennell Who dep^d Novr the 12th 1797 ag^d 50 yrs. Allso her son john fennell Dep^d July the 7th 1789 Ag^d 15 Y^{rs}

Two spellings of the surname appear in the inscription.

Sinnott 1780 Memorial Number 102

The headstone stands 79 cm in height by 64 cm in width and is 4-7 cm in depth.

Iconography:
The crossed I H S Monogram occurs within a rayed circle. An inverted heart and ladder occur to the left and the pincers holding a nail to the right.

The Inscription Reads
Here Lieth the Body of judy Sinnott Died 2^d Octo ^{r} 1780 AG ^{d} 66 Yrs Lord have mercy on her Soul Amen

The 'Passion Symbols' have been a favourite subject of rural Irish headstone cutters since the second quarter of the 18th century. The term simply refers to instruments, from both biblical and traditional sources, used during the crucifixion of Jesus. Denise Maher[24] suggests that the symbols were first used in Ireland on the *Domhnach Airgid* shrine in the mid 14th century. This shrine is now on display in the National Museum. Walton[25] states that the symbols were reintroduced to Ireland in Waterford by the sculptor, William Kidwell in 1711, following their abandonment during the Cromwellian era.

[24]Maher, D. 1997. *Medieval Graveslabs of County Tipperary*, 1200 – 1600. BAR, Oxford.
[25]Walton, Julian C. 1980. Pictorial Decoration on East Waterford Tombstones. *Decies* 14, 67-83.

This small headstone stands 66 cm in height by 53 cm in width by 3-5 cm in depth.

Iconography:

The principal decoration consists of a simple I H S motif surmounted by a cross. Symbols of the passion occur on either side, a pincers holding a nail on the right and a ladder on the left.

The Inscription Reads in Capitals:

HERE LIETH THE BODY OF DENNIS DORCY WHO DEPARTED THIS LIFE ON MARCH 17TH DAY IN OR LORD 1742 AGE 55 YEARS. ALL SO MARGARET DORCY AGED 29 1759.

Based on style and inscription , the headstone of Dennis Dorcy, as the name is inscribed, is likely to date from the 1740s, the second burial being added later. Therefore the stone depicts the earliest passion symbols represented at Kilnahue. This is a well made example of an early vernacular headstone.

The large Breen headstone is leaning forward at an acute angle. Measurements are 123 cm in height, 93 cm in width and 11 cm in depth.

Iconography:

A small crossed I H S motif is set within a rayed circle, which in turn occurs within a decorative *gloria* scroll. These are flanked by a foliate pattern. Large elaborate *ciboria* within domed panels flank the central motif. Quarter sunbursts decorate the upper and lower left corners of the decorated area. Similar ornamentation probably decorated the right side which is now damaged.

The Inscription Reads:

This stone was erected by Michael Breen in memory of his beloved mother Bridget Breen who dep[d] this life Dec 28th 1856 aged 85 years. Here too lies the mortal remains of his brother James Breen deceased April 30th 18 (the stone is damaged at this point) aged 27 years. Also his brother Peter Breen deceased Sept 6th 1840 aged 45 years.

The iconography on the Breen headstone is very representative of the type that became popular during the Post-Famine era.

Higgins 1801 Memorial Number 105

Height: 136 cm
Width: 50 cm
Depth :   8 cm

Iconography:
This tall attractively coloured sandstone memorial displays a large cross extending above the I H S. Two smaller crosses fill the vacant area beneath the cross arms.

The three crosses may represent Calvary, where according to the Gospel accounts, Jesus was crucified between two thieves.

The Inscription Reads in Capitals:
HERE LIES THE BODY OF MILES HIGGINS WHO DEPARTED THIS LIFE APRIL 7TH 1801 AGED 96 YEARS. ALSO HIS WIFE MARY ANN WHO DEPARTED THIS LIFE FEBRARY 6TH AGED 77 . LORD HAVE MERCY ON THEIR SOULS AMEN.

It seems from the above inscription that Miles Higgins and his wife Mary died within 2 months of each other. At 96 years old, Miles Higgins is the second oldest individual whose burial is recorded at Kilnahue. The headstone belongs to the homemade vernacular variety and is similar to those dating from 50 or 60 years earlier. The occurrence of this dated headstone on the site demonstrates the danger of attributing a memorial to a specific narrow time slot, based solely on style. It also indicates how fashion and style may change slowly in rural areas, or indeed that everybody was not interested in the latest trends.

The stone stands 128 cm in height by 95 cm in width and is 7 cm in depth.

The maker's name, A.N. Enniscorthy, is inscribed on the upper right of the decorated area.

Iconography:
The decoration on the Nolen headstone is in poor condition, which is a common feature of most stones depicting the Altar / Tabernacle theme. The mason portrayed a church altar with a tabernacle surmounted by a cross, flanked by candlesticks and candles and framed by a Classical portico. An I H S Monogram is incised on the altar front. Two similar porticos, in which *ciboria* occur, flank the central ornamentation.

The Inscription Reads:
Erect^d by Bridg^t Nolen of Gorey tn in memo^y of her Husb^d Jam^s Nolen who dep^d th^s life May 8th 1828 ag^d 50 yrs

It is sometimes difficult to determine exactly what particular details of the altar / tabernacle theme the stone cutter meant to represent. Tabernacles, church altars and structural facades often displayed the same architectural styles. But as always, it is the symbolism of the decorative display that mattered rather than an accurate illustration.

Uninscribed Memorial Number 107

Height: 64 cm
Width: 34 cm
Depth: 7 cm

There are several inscribed stones at Kilnahue recording burials that took place decades before the headstone was erected. These include the Heydon Memorial Number 41, Laughlin Number 48 and Dunn Number 35. It is reasonable to suggest that there must have been some means of marking those burials prior to the erection of a standard headstone.

For example, the Heydon headstone records the death of a child, Thomas, in 1716, but a quarter century had passed before another family member's burial is recorded. The headstone is roughly contemporary with the second burial.

Further evidence of the practice is provided by the Dunn headstone. The death of Brien Dunn is recorded as having occurred in 1768. The stone is signed by J. Byrne but is cut in a later version of his style. Byrne's early style is represented on the Richmond Memorial Number 123, recording a burial in 1787. Therefore, Byrne, employing his later style, must have cut the Dunn headstone sometime after the second recorded burial in 1789, or perhaps even later, as burials are recorded again in 1798 and in 1807.

It is therefore conceivable that rough stone markers, or indeed home made vernacular headstones, were used to mark these burial places during the intervening years. Some were possibly removed by the family upon erection of an inscribed headstone; others are preserved *in situ*.

Kinsley 1807 Memorial Number 108

This headstone stands 97 cm in height, 96 cm in width and varies between 4 and 6 cm in depth. It leans towards and to the left.

Iconography:

The Kinsley headstone conforms to the Altar / Tabernacle type. The central figure of Christ crucified, overhead crossed I H S and monstrances incorporating the I H S on either side of the crucifixion are clear. Closer inspection reveals two weakly cut figures flanking the cross; these were traditionally, Mary the mother of Jesus and Mary Magdalene. The crucified figure is portrayed within a domed portico. Small *ciboria* occur on each side below the headstone shoulders.

The Inscription Reads:

Here lieth the Body of Pa^{tk} Kinsley of Pallace who Dp^{d} this life Novr 26 1807 Ag^{d} 73 years lord have mercy on his Soul amen.

Kinsela 1787 Memorial Number 109

Height: 112 cm
Width: 72 cm
Depth: 5 – 6 cm

Iconography:

This Kinsela headstone again depicts the Altar / Tabernacle theme. The figure of the crucified Christ is set within a double Classical portico. The I H S motif occurs beneath. Identical altars framed within porticos occur on either side of the central iconography, complete with monstrance and candelabra. A *gloria* scroll extends beneath the iconographic display.

The Inscription Reads:

Here lies the Body of Mary Kinsela who Dep[d] this life March 9th 1787 Aged 78 yr[s]

The tradition of depicting ornamentation and figures within panels is ancient in Irish and Insular art. This practice may be noted on the majority of ancient high crosses and in many early medieval manuscripts including the Books of Durrow, Kells and Lindisfarne. Porticos are not as commonly used, but examples which may have provided inspiration for the headstone carvers, are the Arrest of Christ from the Book of Kells and the Portrait of Saint John from the Canterbury Codex Aureus[26].

It is probable that the best examples of headstones in this category are those by the sculptor, Kehoe at St Mullins, Co. Carlow, which date from the early 19th century[27].

---

[26] Nordenfalf, C. 1995. *Celtic and Anglo-Saxon Painting.* George Braziller, New York.

[27] Longfield, A. 1948. Some Late 18th and Early 19th Century Irish Tombstones. Subjects not related to the Crucifixion. Saints and Scenes by Kehoe, at St. Mullins and by an unknown carver, at Termonfeckin. *Journal of the Royal Society of Antiquaries of Ireland* 77, 1-4.

The Stanton headstone stands 156 cm in height by 89 cm in width. It is circa 5 cm in depth.

Iconography:

Decorative detail on the Stanton headstone is lost. However, it is more than likely another example of a stone displaying the Altar / Tabernacle theme. There is a faint outline of a portico and, based on the setting of the three I H S motifs, it is likely that the original design was similar to that of the Dooley Monument Number 58 which displayed monstrance in this area.

The Inscription Reads:

Here lieth the Body of Robert Stanton who Dep this life Sep 3rd 1811 Age 38 years. Erected by Michael Stanton his son.

May he rest in peace Amen is inscribed at the base of the stone.

Uninscribed Iron Memorial Number 111

Height:	86 cm
Width:	43 cm
Depth:	2 cm

This forged iron cross is set in a concrete plinth measuring 28 cm by 15 cm by 10 cm in height. There is no inscription or maker's name apparent.

Of the three iron 'Celtic' crosses at Kilnahue, this is the smallest. It also differs from the others in style, and may be more correctly termed 'a ringed bracelet cross'. But there is no reason to suggest that it is not near contemporary with both the stone and iron 'Celtic Revivalist' style memorials on the site.

Although the vast majority of burial memorials were of stone, other materials were also used. At Kilnahue most of the older headstones are of sandstone, the most notable exceptions being the six early granite stones, three older limestones, the 1759 shale example Number 69 and the cross-slab like uninscribed Memorial Number 68, made also of shale. Many of the later headstones, particularly in the 'Celtic Revivalist' style are of limestone; two of the 'Celtic Revivalist' memorials are of white marble.

Iron crosses are reasonably common throughout the country. It is regrettable that the maker of the Kilnahue examples did not identify himself. An Iron example at Mothel, Co Waterford, was inscribed by Houlihan of Tinhalla, a well known family of blacksmiths in the area. Interestingly, the crossed I H S motif on Houlihan's own limestone 1807 memorial at Mothel is formed from chain links, an obvious reference to the blacksmith trade.

Timber crosses were also used and are still to be seen in some areas. Perhaps wooden crosses were more common prior to the introduction of stone memorials. Burgess, in his *English Churchyard Memorials* (page 117), refers to some 17th and 18th century examples which survive in the south east of England, but in a poor state of preservation.

Illegible Memorial Number 112

The headstone stands 105 cm in height, 67 cm in width and is 12 cm in depth

This granite example displays the usual I H S motif surmounted by a cross. This decoration covers the upper 26 cm of the stone.

In common with four of the six other granite headstones at Kilnahue, the inscription is currently illegible. It is impossible to date the headstone with certainty, but based on its proximity to the dated granite Number 113 and on its probable employment of capital letters, it seems likely that both stones are contemporary. It was noted on the site that roughly contemporary headstones are often adjacent and display some common features. Examples are Numbers 13 and 14, Numbers 34 and 35, Numbers 74, 75, 76 and 77.

Byrne 1741 and 1757 Memorial Number 113

Height:	82 cm
Width:	65 cm
Depth:	12 cm

Iconography:

A large I H S Motif surmounted by a cross occupies the lunette on this granite headstone. The inscription occurs within a chamfered panel below.

The Inscription Reads in Capitals:

HERE LIETH THE BODY OF TERENCE BYRNE WHO DEPARTED THIS LIFE IN THE YEAR 1757 AGE 29. JAMES BYRNE 1741 AGED 18

There are several surnames at Kilnahue that are today commonly found using the prefix 'O'. These include Toole, Laughlin, Kelley, Donohoe and Hanlon, as well as the numerous Byrne and Connor examples and the less numerous Nolan and Sheridan. Only Memorial Number 59, that of Thomas O'Neill in 1799, uses the 'O' prefix. MacLysaght[28] illustrates how only 4% of those with the name Sullivan used the 'O' in 1866. By 1944 this had risen to 60%. However, the use of the prefix by O'Neill families never fell below 50%.

---

[28]MacLysaght, E. 2007. *The Surnames of Ireland*. Irish Academic Press, Dublin. Page xi

Byrn 1769 Memorial Number 114

Height: 125 cm
Width: 62 cm
Depth: 8 cm

Iconography:
The crucified Christ occurs as the central decorative motif. On the right Cullen has portrayed the centurion on horseback as usual; he is dressed in 18th century uniform and holds a musket in his raised hand. Between the centurion and the cross, a faint figure represents Mary the mother of Jesus, identified by her crown. The lance bearer is set on the left, together with a winged angel. A reference to Peter's denial of Christ on the previous day is represented by a cock perched on a pillar The sun, with a human face in the centre, representing 'Glory' occurs in the lower left corner.

This headstone is signed by the mason, Dennis Cullen.

The Inscription Reads:
Here Lyeth the Body of Daniell Byrn Who Departed this Life ye 21st of August 1769 Ag^d 36 y'ars.

In Ireland, archaeology is legally defined as the study of the material remains of past societies. By studying headstone iconography and inscriptions, archaeologists may learn something of the cultural, social, religious and economic values of the society that produced them. Cullen's depiction of Roman soldiers dressed in modern uniform and holding muskets is interesting. Did 18th century society view events from the past in a contemporary context, or was Cullen being subtly political? Perhaps he was simply using artistic license.

In Renaissance art biblical events were routinely depicted as contemporary with the Medieval world.

This headstone stands 97 cm in height by 79 cm in width and is 8 cm in depth.

This headstone is signed beneath the decoration by the manufacturer, J. Nolan, Ferns.

Iconography:

An I H S motif occurs surmounted by a cross within a rayed circle. A large *gloria* scroll extends across the face of the stone. Central decoration is flanked by ornate *ciboria* within domed panels.

The Inscription Reads:

Here lies the body of Christiph^r Connor late of barnland who dep^d this life the 25 th of May 1831 Aged 36 years. Also his father Bryan Connor die 7 th March 1821 Aged 80 years also his Mother Mary Connor the 8 th of Jan 1831 Aged 87 years.

The manufacturer's name, M. Grannan, Gorey, is inscribed at the base of the memorial.

The Travers headstone stands 214 cm in height by 96 cm in width and is 10 cm in depth. A nearby tree is beginning to envelop the stone.

Iconography:

Iconography consists of the Lamb of God lying on a cross beneath the I H S Monogram. This decoration is flanked by paneled *ciboria*.

The Inscription Reads:

Erected by Thomas Travers Gorey in memory of His father James Travers who dep[d] this life 18 th Sept 1871 Aged 75 Years. Also His Four Brothers and 2 Sisters who dep[d] this life at a young age. His Mother Anne Travers died 6th May 1888 Aged 87 Years. R.I.P.

Byrne and Mulligan 1812, 1832 and 1867 Memorial Number 117

Height: 168 cm
Width: 59 cm
Depth: 10 cm

This stylized Gothic cross is located in the trees at the western extremity of the churchyard.

Iconography:
The iconography employed portrays the Lamb of God lying on a cross in the centre.

The manufacturer's name, D. Scally and Son Glasnevin, is inscribed at the base.

The Inscription Reads:
Erected by Denis Byrne of Gorey in memory of his beloved Father Patrick Byrne who departed this life 7th August 1832 Aged 72 years. Also his beloved Mother Ann Byrne who departed this life 9th July 1812 Aged 63 years And Four of his Children Patrick Michael Anne and Margaret who died young. Here also repose the remains of his deeply lamented daughter Ellen Mulligan who departed this life 20th Decenber 1867 aged 20 years. May they rest in peace.

Kavanagh Memorial Number 118

This rough stone measures 59 cm in height by 50 cm in width and is 12 cm in depth. The stone is situated in the grove at the western extremity of the churchyard.

The Inscription Reads:

J. Kavanagh

The short inscription is roughly and lightly etched. It is not usual to find a name on a rough stone of this type; conceivably the etching was protected by the memorial's location within the grove. However, roughly incised initials also occurred on Memorial Number 2. Perhaps similar inscriptions have been weathered away on stones located in more exposed areas.

It is difficult to determine with certainty how families and neighbours recognized burial plots prior to the introduction of inscriptions. But then, this would not have mattered in an illiterate society. Perhaps different shaped stones were purposely selected to aid plot identification. The sample of the various rough stones was chosen with a view towards illustrating this point. Memorial Number 19 is triangular, Number 92 is rectangular, Number 99 is tall and angular and Number 107 is tall and rounded.

Donohoe 1880 and 1883 Memorial Number 119

Height:	176 cm
Width:	77 cm
Depth:	10 cm

This memorial is located in the grove at the western extremity of the churchyard.

Iconography:
This is another 'Celtic' style ringed cross of the late 19th century. A large I H S motif occurs as the central decoration and a small stylized cross decorates each of the four cross arms.

The manufacturer's name, M. Travers, Gorey, is incised at the base of the stone.

The Inscription Reads:
Erected by Daniel Donohoe of Gorey in memory of his Beloved Wife Mary Anne Donohoe who depd this life 5 June 1880 aged 75 years Also His three Children who died young. Also the above Daniel Donohoe died 10th Fb 1883 Aged 84 years. R.I.P.

Late 19th and early 20th century headstones at Kilnahue are dominated by those manufactured by Travers of Gorey. There are twelve in total: Numbers 4, 5, 8, 18, 20, 21, 31, 32, 52, 53, 119, and 124. Most are very similar and conform to contemporary fashion. They also tend to occur in small isolated groups within the churchyard, which might indicate how choice of headstone was influenced during this period. In general, headstones tend to be similar in style to those located in close proximity.

Travers 1866, 1880 and 1882 Memorial Number 120

Height:	172 cm
Width:	79 cm
Depth:	10 cm

Iconography:

A stylized Maltese type cross occurs within a ribboned cross as the central motif. This is flanked by ornate *ciboria* within Gothic panels.

The Inscription Reads:

Erected by Margaret Travers in Memory of her beloved Father Mathew Travers of Tinashina who departed this life 15th March 1866 aged 55 years her Brother Mathew died 6th Dec 1880 aged 40 yrs her Mother Catherine died Feb 28 1882 Aged 80 years Also the above Margaret Travers died 5th June 1882 aged 45 yrs. Requiescant in Pace

A passage from the Second Book of Maccabees, Chapter 12, Verse 46, is inscribed on the back of the headstone within a large lightly incised cross. The same quotation is noted on the reverse of Monument Number 97.

It is a Holy and Wholesome thought to pray for the dead that they may be loosed from their sins. 2. Mac. XII. 46

Connor and Redmond 1864, 1870, 1881, 1891 and 1903
Memorial Number 121

Height:	146 cm
Width:	90 cm
Depth:	5cm

Iconography:

The Connor headstone repeats a decorative pattern that had not been used at Kilnahue since c. 1830. A very stylized Altar / Tabernacle scene is depicted within a domed portico beneath a crossed I H S motif. A cross also lies at the foot of the proposed altar. Monstrance and two ciboria, one big and one small, occur at either side of the principal decoration.

The manufacturer's name, T. Cosgrave, John St, Wex, is centrally inscribed beneath the decoration.

The Inscription Reads:

Erected by James Connor of Templederry in memory of his wife Mrs mary connor alias Redmond who dep^d this life May 13th 1864 in the 69th year of her age. Also the above James Connor who depd this life July 12th 1870 aged 86 Years. Also his daughter Catherine died 26th April 1881 aged 60 yrs. Also his daughter Mary died 14th Jan 1891 age 69 yrs. Also his son James died 22 Jan 1903 age 72 yrs.

May her soul rest in peace is inscribed at the base, indicating that the headstone was erected in the 1860s prior to the death of James Connor in 1870.

The reverse, or west facing side of the headstone, depicts an incised cross on a plinth. It also carries a short request to those who read it:

Christians dear I crave, Our prayer from you, For me that lie in this silent grave, Our Father, Hail Mary

The Connor headstone measures 138 cm in height by 82 cm in width and is 9 cm in depth.

This headstone is signed by the mason, D. Toole, above the inscription on the upper left.

Iconography:

Decoration consists of a plain I H S motif surmounted by a cross occurring within a rayed circle.

The Inscription Reads:

Erected by Michael Connor of Belcarrig in Memory of his Wife Catherine Connor otherwise Roche who Died the 16th of June 1809 Aged 59 Yrs Lord have Mercy on her Soul amen.

There are two headstones by the mason, D. Toole at Kilnahue: the above and Memorial Number 43. Both are somewhat similar.

The Richmond headstone measures 84 cm in height by 78 cm in width by 5 cm in depth. It is located in shrubbery in the north western section of the site.

The mason J. Byrne has signed the headstone on the right beneath the inscription.

Iconography:
The figure of the crucified Christ is depicted in the centre. Two male figures dressed in 18th century military costume stand on the right. The lance bearer is portrayed on the left in the act of piercing Jesus' side. A damaged figure stands behind him. The I H S Monogram is incised beneath the crucifix.

The Inscription Reads:
Here lies the Body of John Richmond who Dep[d] this life June 6th 1787 AG[d] 25 Y[rs] Lord have Mercy on his So[ul]

It is unusual to find the mason's signature beneath the inscription. This is an early example of Byrne's work; it seems that he was very influenced by Cullen prior to developing his own style.

Woodroofe 1900 Memorial Number 124

Height: 150 cm
Width: 61 cm
Depth: 8 cm

This burial is located within the grove of trees in the north eastern section of the site.

Iconography:

On this 'Celtic Revivalist' type memorial, the Lamb of God lying on a cross occurs as a central motif within a diamond shaped panel. The shamrock, formed of inlaid lead, is displayed on each of the four cross arms.

The manufacturer's name, Travers, Gorey, is inscribed near the base of the memorial.

The Inscription Reads:

Erected by Richard Woodroofe of Gorey in memory of his wife Mary Woodroofe who died 17th Jan 1900 aged 45 years. R.I.P

The Woodroofe headstone is very similar in style to that of Numbers 4 and 5. But there are some minor differences. The memorial is now being forced forward by the trees behind it. It is probable that they were planted shortly after the stone's erection.

Doyle 1851, 1876 and 1887 Memorial Number 125

This ledger measures 248 cm in length by 122 cm in width by 12 cm in depth.

Iconography:

Decoration consists of a small crossed I H S motif above the inscription.

The Inscription Reads:

Erected by Thos Doyle if Ballinastraw in memory of his beloved Wife Elizabeth Doyle who dep^d this life Octr 10th 1851 aged 66 years Also the above Thos Doyle dep^d this life May 8 1876 Aged 80 years. His son James Doyle died 1887 aged 53. Requisecant in Pace Amen

Only two ledger type memorials and one table tomb were recorded at Kilnahue. This does not represent a particularly high number when compared to other parts of the country.

Fallen Memorial Number 126

Height: 186 cm
Width: 75 cm
Depth: 8 cm

This headstone has fallen face downwards in the churchyard.

It was not the mission of this survey to interfere in any way with the memorials or with the position in which they are currently located. Therefore, all recordings reflect the state of the churchyard and the condition of the stones, their iconography and their inscriptions, during 2010.

In recent years, particularly as a result of the upsurge of interest in genealogical studies, medieval parish churchyards have witnessed more visitors than at any time since their days of common usage. By far the majority of visitors respect these sites and leave them in the condition in which they were found. However, others are somewhat over enthusiastic in their efforts to read the stones and can inflict permanent damage on them in pursuit of genealogical information. Some of the unwelcome practices employed include the use of chemicals or of sandblasting to 'clean' the stones.

Since the 1994 National Monuments Amendment Act there is a legal obligation on any group carrying out conservation or any other kind of work in burial grounds to do so only in accordance with the advice of a qualified person, generally an archaeologist licensed by The Department of the Environment, Heritage and Local Government. Any disturbance to the site or its grounds is illegal without a license from the same department. A booklet, *The Care and Conservation of Graveyards*, is available from the Government Sales Office, Molesworth Street, Dublin.

Glossary of the Decorative Motifs at Kilnahue

Symbolism has always played an integral part in art. Indigenous Irish art was no different. But it is probable that past societies had a better understanding of symbols than that generally found among modern populations. It is intended here to briefly identify and explain the symbolism on the Kilnahue headstones. Because the decorative motifs employed are dealing with death and a resurrection hope it tends to have religious associations, a theme common to the vast majority of Irish headstones.

The Cross: The cross has become one of the most familiar symbols in Christian art. It symbolizes Jesus' pain in taking unto himself the sins of the world rather than physical suffering. The Plain Cross, sometimes referred to as The Resurrection Cross, predates the crucifixion portrayal in Christian art.

The Crucified Christ: The figure of the crucified Christ was never displayed in Christian art prior to the 5th century. Until the 11th century the figure was always displayed fully clothed.

The 'Celtic' Cross: The revival of the 'Celtic Cross' is noted to occur during the second half of the 19th century. It is probable that interest was generated by an exhibition of Medieval Irish high cross plaster replicas in Dublin in 1853. All crosses in this category at Kilnahue date to the late 19th and early 20th centuries. It is likely that the three un-dated forged iron crosses on site are near contemporary. The popularity of the high cross replicas was no doubt further enhanced by the publication in 1887 of Margaret Stokes' *Early Christian Art in Ireland*. This was a period of general Gaelic revival, which also gave rise to the Land League, the G.A.A., *Conradh na Gaeilge* and several nationalist political organisations.

I H S Motif: This motif is generally referred to as 'The Monogram'. Reference is to the first three letters in the Greek version of Jesus' name, *Ihsous*, written in Latin as *Iesus Homien Salvador*, meaning Jesus the Saviour of Mankind. The overhead cross developed from the practice of inscribing a stroke above the Monogram indicating its abbreviation, crossing the vertical bar of the h.

I.N.R.I: According to the Gospel (John, 19: 19), 'Pilate also wrote a title and put it on the cross; it read 'Jesus of Nazareth, the King of the Jews', or in Latin. *Iesus Nazarenus Rex Iudaeorum*, giving the abbreviation I N R I.

Gloria Scroll: The Latin phrase, *Gloria in Excelsis Deo*, translates as Glory to God in the Highest. The *Gloria* was part of the old Latin Mass but was omitted from masses for the dead and on All Soul's Day. According to the Gospels it was sung by the heavenly host at the Birth of Christ (Luke 2: 14). This might be an indication that the symbol was associated with re-birth and resurrection rather than with death.

Monstrance: The Sacred Host was displayed on the altar, or during procession, in a monstrance. It occurs on early 19th century headstones at Kilnahue.

The Moon Crescent: During the Middle Ages the moon was thought to be the abode of the Archangel Gabriel, accounting for the inclusion of a face on the symbol[29]. It is commonly found on headstones depicting the Passion of Christ.

The Sun: The sun is sometimes portrayed on the Passion Symbol headstones with a face in the centre. During the Medieval period this symbol represented 'Glory'[30], and may symbolize a future resurrection hope based on Christ's sacrifice. However, the sun, moon and stars are usually depicted on the Passion Symbol headstones of the Kilsheelan / Kilmurry group. This might be in acknowledgement of the passage in the Gospel of St Luke 23: 44, 'It was now the sixth hour, and there was darkness over the whole land until the ninth hour'.

Ciborium: A *ciborium* is generally larger that a chalice and is distinguished by having a lid, usually surmounted by a cross. In it are contained the hosts, which may symbolise a resurrection hope for those interred beneath.

Sacred Heart: The Heart of Jesus, sometimes pierced by arrows, is occasionally found beneath the I H S Monogram on headstones from the 18th century onwards. During the latter half of the 19th century the Sacred Heart developed as a central motif. It symbolises the love of Jesus for humanity whilst suffering for the sins of the world. The adoration of the Sacred Heart spread throughout the Catholic world following the claimed visions of the French Saint, Margaret Mary Alacoque, in the late 17th century.

The Lamb of God: The lamb is portrayed on burial memorials from the mid 19th century onwards and sometimes occurs as a central motif on 'Celtic Crosses'. Reference is to the biblical prophesy of Isaiah (53: 7) 'like a lamb he was led to the slaughter'. Therefore the symbol is usually depicted in association with the cross. The *Agnus Dei*, or Lamb of God, was also one of the preparatory prayers before communion in the Latin Mass.

The Rayed Circle: The *Corona Radiata* has associations with the sun and some mythological gods. This motif transcended both eastern and western cultures and came to symbolise divine and human power in the person of kings and emperors. It was later adopted by Christianity and used extensively to illustrate holiness or divinity in Early and Later Medieval art[31]. In Ireland the symbol is found on headstones of all periods radiating from the central I H S Monogram. It occurs in varying forms and degrees of ornamentation.

---

[29] Hulme, E. 1976. *Symbolism in Christian Art*. Blandford, Poole. Page 206
[30] Mollett, J.W. 1883 (1994). *Dictionary of Art and Archaeology*. Bracken Books, London. Page 308.
[31] Hulme pages 57 – 58, 88 – 90

Floral Motifs: It has been suggested[32] that the laurel wreath worn by Roman Emperors had its origin in the *Corona Radiata,* and that the Crown of Thorns worn by Christ was in fact a mockery of that symbol. A foliate or floral pattern sometimes replaced the rayed circle that encompassed the central motif, or occurred independently.

Cherubs: Cherubs are not as commonly found on Irish headstones as they are on British and North American examples. In New England it is suggested that the cherub may represent a likeness of the deceased[33]. Again, in common with other decorative motifs, there may be a biblical and resurrection theme involved. According to Genesis 3: 24; cherubs were placed to guard the Tree of Life in the Garden of Eden after the expulsion of Adam and Eve.

Spirals: Only the headstone of Margaret Bready, 1761 (Memorial Number 16), displayed a spiral motif. This form of decoration is well known in Irish and Insular art and is commonly found in Passage Tombs of the Neolithic period. A similar spiral to that depicted on the Bready headstone occurs on the North Cross at Ahenny, Co. Tipperary, and on the Cross Base at Tibberaghny, Co Kilkenny, possibly indicating the mason's interest and awareness of his tradition and that he had travelled in the course of his work.

Whorl Motif: Whorls have usually been associated with 'Celtic' style art and at Kilnahue occur on the 'Celtic Revivalist' headstone of Hobbs Memorial Number 4.

Symbols of the Passion of Christ: The various symbols of the Passion of Christ were commonly depicted on Irish headstones from the second quarter of the 18th century onwards. The term refers to the instruments used during the crucifixion of Christ and may include the cross, lance, ladder, hammer, nails and pincers. Associated biblical references include the dice, thirty pieces of silver, scourge and crown of thorns. Artistic style varies throughout the country. The headstones of the un-named Kilmurry / Kilsheelan mason located in South Tipperary, South Kilkenny and North County Waterford are noted for their variety of instruments. The Hickey 1756 headstone at Rathgormack, County Waterford, is a typical example. The crucified Christ, ladder, lance, a cock crowing on a pillar, representing Peter's denial, dice, dice box, sponge, a bucket holding a hammer and pincers, scourge and rope, thirty silver coins, a bag for the coins, moon and stars, a tomb with the stone rolled away, a staff, a chalice collecting the blood, a garment and a reed sceptre, are all illustrated floating within a very confined space.

Occasionally the peacock may be noted among the symbols and is easily confused with the representation of the cock and pillar. In Roman mythology the peacock was represented bearing the empress to heaven. Christianity adopted it as a symbol of the resurrection.

---

[32] Hulme, page 90.
[33] Dethlefsen, E. and Deetz, J. 1966. Death's Heads, Cherubs and Willow Trees: experimental archaeology in colonial cemeteries. *American Antiquity 31* (4), 502 – 10

The crucifixion, temple, tomb, ladder, hammer, nails, pincers and lance are the most common passion symbols noted at Kilnahue. A dice occurs once.

The Temple: Many of the Passion Symbol headstones at Kilnahue depict an image of the temple, sometimes illustrated as a contemporary church. Its portrayal in this context is likely to refer to Jesus' prophesy in the Gospel of St John (2: 19), 'destroy this temple and in three days I will raise it up'. According to Christian teaching, Jesus was referring to himself and to his forthcoming resurrection, obviously a fitting theme for a headstone.

Placenames Referenced on the Kilnahue Memorials

Placename	Family Name(s)	Headstone Number
Inchicore, Dublin	Hobbs	3
Gorey	Hobbs	4
Gorey	Hobbs	5
Gorey	Webb	8
Clogue and Coleshall	Nolan and Byrne	12
Gorey	Cullen	17
Creagh	Fitzsimons and Fitzgerald	18
Gorey	Byrne	20
Gorey Hill	Byrne	21
Gorey Hill	Sheridan and Byrne	31
Creagh	Byrne	32
Ballygarrett	Redmond and Byrne	37
Bishop St, Dublin	Sinnott and Davis	43
B^{l}Clash, Co Wicklow	Byrne	44
Gowrey	Darcy and Flusk	46
Creagh	Kenna	52
Creagh	Fitzsimons	53
Toreduff	Cullen	79
Gorey	Murphy	94
Castletown	Hanlon	95
Gorey	Nicholoson	97
Gorey	Nolen	106
Pallace	Kinsley	108
Barnland	Connor	115
Gorey	Travers	116
Gorey	Byrne and Mulligan	117
Gorey	Donohoe	119
Tinashina	Travers	120
Templederry	Connor	121
Belcarrig	Connor and Roche	122
Gorey	Woodroofe	124
Ballinastraw	Doyle	125

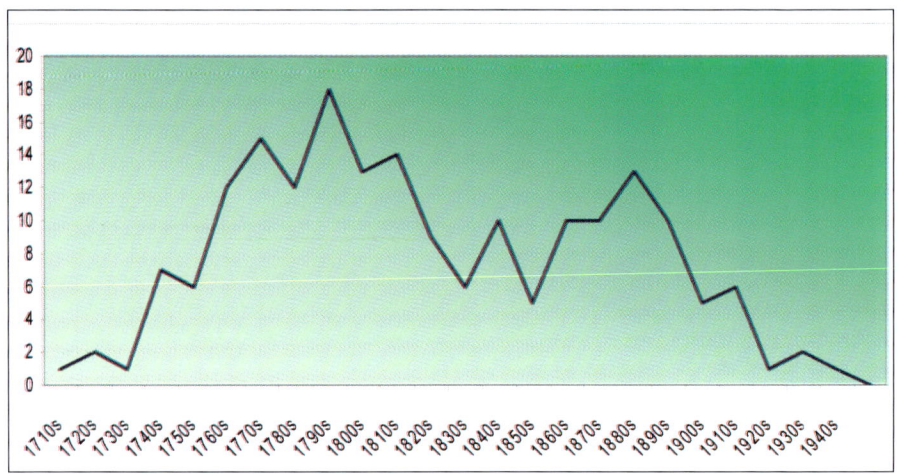

Temporal spread of recorded burials at Kilnahue

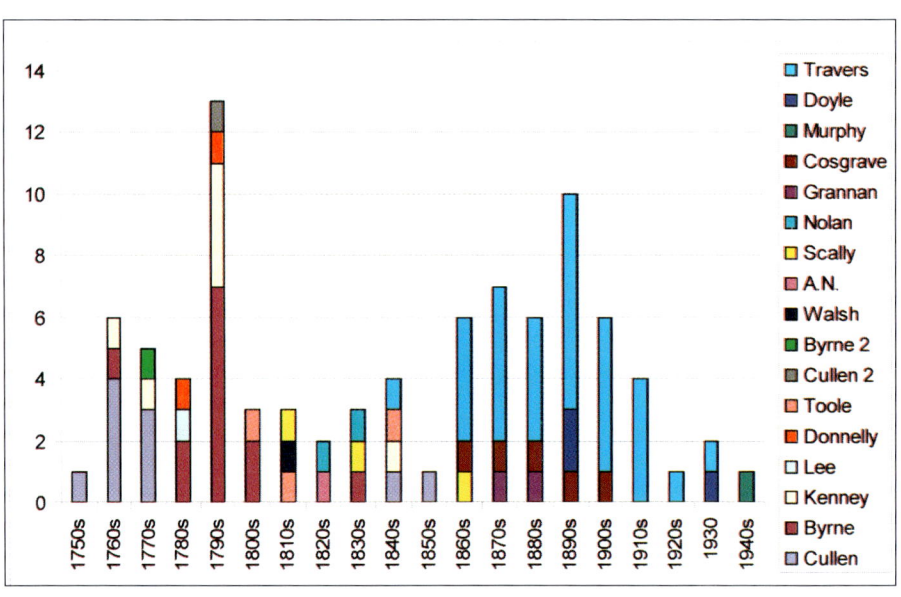

Temporal spread of recorded burials beneath the signed memorials at Kilnahue

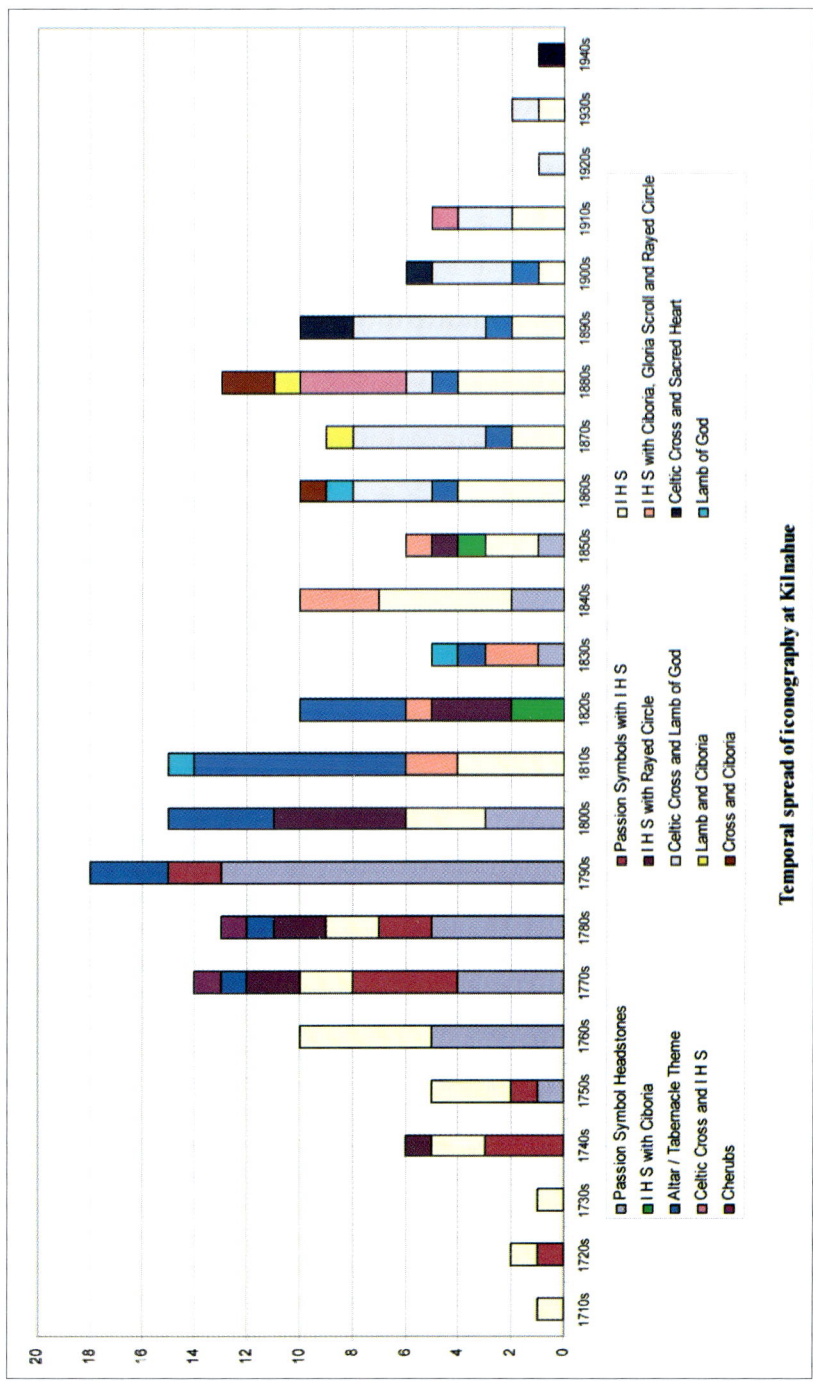

Temporal spread of iconography at Kilnahue